A Model Discipline

A Model Discipline

Political Science and
the Logic of Representations

KEVIN A. CLARKE

AND

DAVID M. PRIMO

OXFORD
UNIVERSITY PRESS

OXFORD
UNIVERSITY PRESS

Oxford University Press, Inc., publishes works that further
Oxford University's objective of excellence
in research, scholarship, and education.

Oxford   New York
Auckland   Cape Town   Dar es Salaam   Hong Kong   Karachi
Kuala Lumpur   Madrid   Melbourne   Mexico City   Nairobi
New Delhi   Shanghai   Taipei   Toronto

With offices in
Argentina   Austria   Brazil   Chile   Czech Republic   France   Greece
Guatemala   Hungary   Italy   Japan   Poland   Portugal   Singapore
South Korea   Switzerland   Thailand   Turkey   Ukraine   Vietnam

Copyright © 2012 by Oxford University Press

Published by Oxford University Press, Inc.
198 Madison Avenue, New York, New York 10016
www.oup.com

Oxford is a registered trademark of Oxford University Press

Library of Congress Cataloging-in-Publication Data

Clarke, Kevin A.
A model discipline : political science and the logic of representations /
Kevin A. Clarke and David M. Primo.
    p. cm.
Includes bibliographical references and index.
ISBN 978-0-19-538219-8 (hardback) – ISBN 978-0-19-538220-4 (pbk.)
1. Political science–Methodology. I. Primo, David M. II. Title.
JA71.C528 2011
320–dc22   2011015267

9   8   7   6   5   4   3   2   1

Printed in the United States of America
on acid-free paper

For Heather and for Neeta

CONTENTS

This book project began with a question raised by an undergraduate student: Why test deductive models? The question seemed simple, even obvious, but after thinking it through, we decided that it was not so simple. A few years earlier, the Empirical Implications of Theoretical Models (EITM) project had gotten under way, and finding new ways to test theoretical models was all the rage. We felt that a paper exploring the logic of testing theoretical models was in order. After writing that paper, we felt that we had more to say, not only about theoretical models but also about empirical models and the conditions under which the two should be combined. This book is the result.

Many people helped us revise, refine, and improve our argument from its initial incarnation. Sometimes we disagreed with the advice that we received, and sometimes the advice givers disagreed among themselves. Thus, all errors are ours, and ours alone.

Among our colleagues at the University of Rochester, we are particularly indebted to Jim Johnson, who supported this work from the beginning, patiently engaged in seemingly endless conversations about models in political science, and who was gracious enough to read a number of drafts. John Duggan, Mark Fey, Hein Goemans, Gretchen Helmke, Bethany Lacina, Michael Peress, Larry Rothenberg, Curt Signorino, and Randy Stone also provided helpful comments and advice. Our arguments have been sharpened by exchanging views with Rochester graduate students both in seminars and in hallways. Outside the department, we benefited from interactions with Chris Achen, Jim

Alt, Neal Beck, Jake Bowers, Henry Brady, Bear Braumoeller, Randy Calvert, Wendy Tam Cho, Doug Dion, Justin Esarey, Rob Franzese, John Freeman, Gary Goertz, Miriam Golden, Jim Granato, John Jackson, Keith Krehbiel, Skip Lupia, Andrew Martin, Scott de Marchi, Becky Morton, Bob Pahre, Kevin Quinn, Jim Snyder, Jonathan Wand, and Alan Zuckerman. Matt Jacobsmeier assisted us with research, and Heather Edes provided painstaking copyediting. There is no doubt that we missed thanking someone despite our best efforts. We hope those that fall into this category forgive us.

Earlier versions of the manuscript were presented to the Political Science Department at Washington University in St. Louis (March 2009), the Directions in Political Methodology Conference at Emory University (November 2010), and a symposium at the University of Illinois (January 2011). Too many individuals to name offered helpful comments and criticisms on these occasions; we thank all of them.

The initial version of the book's argument appeared as "Modernizing Political Science: A Model-Based Approach" in *Perspectives on Politics*. Earlier versions of this article were presented at the 2004 Annual Meeting of the American Political Science Association and at the 2005 Annual Meetings of the Midwest Political Science Association and the Canadian Political Science Association. We thank participants at these conferences for their feedback.

We also acknowledge the support and encouragement of our editor at Oxford University Press, David McBride, as well as Caelyn Cobb and the staff at Oxford University Press for their help in putting the manuscript together.

Finally, we thank Heather and Neeta for putting up with the late-night emails, the early morning emails, the telephone calls, the complaints about coauthors, and the hours that went into writing this book.

A Model Discipline

A Model Discipline

Practical economists, who believe themselves to be quite exempt from any methodological influences, are usually slaves of some defunct methodology.

—Economist KEVIN HOOVER

1.1 THE MODEL IN POLITICAL SCIENCE

This book is about how to think about models and the roles they play in our discipline. Models have come to be the dominant feature of modern political science and can be found in every corner of the field.[1] Pick up any recent issue of the top social science journals, and you will find models. Some are mathematical or formal models, and some are computational or algorithmic models. An even greater number are empirical or statistical models, and some are verbal or nonmathematical models. Despite this ubiquity, most political scientists know very little about models, their properties, or how to think about models in a rigorous fashion, even though political scientists are highly skilled at model construction.

Our goal in this book is to provide political scientists with a coherent way of thinking about the models that pervade our discipline. The approach we take is known as the model-based or model-theoretic view, which holds that models, not theories, are the primary units of scientific interest. Models are seen as objects, thus neither true nor false, and are judged by their usefulness for a particular purpose. The standard analogy is to maps, which share many of the characteristic traits of models. We develop the implications of this understanding and establish why existing practice is based on outdated and faulty ideas. Most political scientists, we suspect, will raise few objections to thinking about models in the way we suggest. That being said, we also suspect that resistance will begin when the consequences of this approach dictate jettisoning cherished pieces of our research tradition. These include the notions that theoretical models must be tested to be of value and that the ultimate goal of empirical analysis is theory testing.

Consider Baron and Ferejohn's (1989) legislative bargaining model, in which a dollar is distributed among legislators interested in maximizing their share. The game begins when a randomly chosen legislator makes a proposal to divide a fixed amount of public expenditures. In the simplest form of the game, if an offer is rejected, a new proposer is chosen, and the process continues until an agreement is reached. The Baron and Ferejohn legislature comprises n members, a recognition rule (random — every member has the same chance of being recognized to make a proposal), an amendment rule (open or closed), and a voting rule (majority). The legislature depicted in the model shares little isomorphism, structural or otherwise, with any existing legislature. There are no parties, no leadership, no disputes over social policy or even debates about the size of overall spending. The benefits are distributed only once. Despite these departures from reality, we clearly recognize the model as being that of a legislature.

Baron and Ferejohn's model cannot be considered either true or false. The model represents some features of actual legislatures and omits others. Moreover, the omissions are purposeful. In constructing the model, the authors sought in part to highlight the roles that proposal power, endogenous agenda formation, and the sequential nature of the legislative process play in the distribution of resources. To that end, the model focuses on proposal rights and amendment rules at the expense of other real-world features of legislatures. The way to think about this modeling effort is to say that Baron and Ferejohn use their model to represent actual legislatures for the purpose of understanding bargaining in the legislative process.[2]

Reasonable people can disagree about whether the representation is useful—the model may be unilluminating, for example—but truth and falsity, and therefore testing, are beside the point. That being said, it is difficult for anyone to argue that the model has not been useful; it spawned a large body of literature and, according to the Social Sciences Citation Index at the time of writing, has been cited over 300 times.

Even if one accepts the misguided notion that theoretical models can be true or false, we demonstrate that the method we use to test theoretical models—derive a comparative static from a model and see if it holds in a regression-like statistical model—does not actually work. There are two reasons. First, the logic of the test prevents us from drawing interesting conclusions about the theoretical model. Second, we never test theoretical models with data; we test theoretical models with models of data. As data models share all the same characteristics of theoretical models and are often exceedingly fragile, assigning the data model to be the final arbiter of the theoretical model is untenable.

Theoretical model testing, in our view, is illogical; moveover, it is often unnecessary. Models can be useful in different ways without being tested. There are foundational models upon which others build, organizational models that collect empirical generalizations under a single framework, exploratory models that investigate putative causal mechanisms, and models that predict. With the exception of predictive models, none of the other uses require testing. Similarly, empirical models can be useful in the absence of theoretical models for measurement, characterizing a data set, and prediction. Two threads, therefore, comprise the argument: model testing is illogical, and model testing is often superfluous.

Our collective ignorance of the nature of models no doubt strikes many political scientists as unproblematic; after all, the ability of social scientists to construct models of precision and elegance is paramount. Increasingly, however, models are being used in ways that are antithetical to their nature. Ask a political scientist if her model is true or false, and she will most likely reply that her model is false. Conventional wisdom holds that all models are false. Ask the same political scientist why she is testing her model, and a reply is likely to be much slower in coming. The initial response is often to make a claim such as "we are not testing the model, but what comes out of it," or "the model is technically false, but it is a good enough approximation," or "well, we are not really *testing* per se." These half-formed arguments just generate additional questions and confusions. Why would we be interested in the implications of a false model? Are the implications of all models approximations? What does that mean for data analysis? If we are not testing the model, why is the deductive connection between the theoretical model and the empirical model necessary?

The true importance of these topics becomes readily apparent when we consider graduate teaching. Broadly speaking, methodology is the study of the ways in which political scientists justify their conclusions about the world (Blaug 1992). We are teaching a generation of top graduate students that there is a preferred way of making substantive claims. The method we teach, however, cannot be justified. It is based on outdated ideas and fails the test of logic; there is no evidence that its use has moved the field forward. Our goal is to help political scientists reach better justified conclusions by highlighting the use of models and by thinking carefully about what models can and cannot do for us.

1.2 METAPHORS AND ANALOGIES, FABLES AND FICTIONS

Before going any further, it will prove useful to put our conception of models into context by reviewing some of the different ways modern scholars have thought about scientific models. Central to any discussion of models is the idea of representation, and central to the idea of representation is use. The act of representing lies not in any necessary physical resemblance between a model and what it purports to represent, but in the way the model is used. Van Fraassen (2008, 23) writes, "There is no representation except in the sense that some things are used, made, or taken, to represent some things as thus or so." Even a novel about animals can represent a political system. George Orwell's *Animal Farm* can be read either as a fantastical story of animals taking over a farm or as an allegory for the events leading to Stalinism (Godfrey-Smith 2009). Whether the novel represents Russia in the early twentieth century depends on the interaction between intention and use.

Modern treatments of scientific models go back to Black's (1962) seminal discussion of models as metaphors. Black begins with *scale* models, by which he means three-dimensional versions of objects that have been scaled either down (as in a model ship) or up (as in a model of an atom). The objects being modeled may be real (such as the Space Shuttle Endeavour) or imagined (such as models of spaceships from movies or television shows). These kinds of models are designed to serve specific purposes that range from the pedagogical to entertainment, and depending on the use, some features of the original are important to the representation whereas others are irrelevant. A child would find a model airplane that could not fly quite dull, whereas an adult collector would not care less, provided the model sported authentic detail. Either way, the change of scale must introduce distortion, and it follows that "perfectly faithful" models do not exist. A model can represent "only by being unfaithful in *some* respect" (Black 1962, 220).[3]

Black moves toward the types of models used in political science when he writes of *analogue* models in which an object is represented in some new medium. Whereas a scale model shares features with its original, an analogue model shares only a structure or pattern of relationships. A subset of analogue models are mathematical models through which structures are represented in the new medium of mathematics. Black (1962, 223–24) writes of the use of mathematical models in the social sciences in a way familiar to any political scientist (at least until the last sentence):

> The original field is thought of as "projected" upon the abstract domain of sets, functions, and the like that is the subject matter of the correlated mathematical theory; thus social forces are said to be "modeled" by relations between mathematical entities. The "model" is conceived to be *simpler* and *more abstract* than

the original. Often there is a suggestion of the model's being a kind of ethereal analogue model, as if the mathematical equations referred to an invisible mechanism whose operation illustrates or even partially explains the operation of the original social system under investigation. This last suggestion must be rejected as an illusion.

Theoretical models, according to Black (1962, 230), stand in relation to their originals in the same way that analogue models and their originals do. That is, the theoretical model represents the structure of the original. Black describes such models as metaphors with the power to bring "two separate domains into cognitive and emotional relation" by using the language of one as "a lens for seeing the other" (236–37). Like models, metaphors may fit well or not, and the outcome of metaphorical thinking is unpredictable; the metaphor may help the scientist see new connections.

An idea closely related to the view of models as metaphors is that of models as analogies, which are often important in understanding metaphors (Bailer-Jones 2009). Hesse (1966), drawing on the work of Campbell (1920), makes the models are analogies argument and illustrates her approach with an example from the dynamical theory of gases: gas molecules are analogous to billiard balls. The analogy has three components. The positive analogy contains the properties of billiard balls that are shared with gas molecules. The negative analogy contains the properties of billiard balls that are not shared by gas molecules. The neutral analogy contain those properties of billiard balls that are unknown or cannot be classified as positive or negative. A model can be either physical, such as the billiard balls, or mathematical. Hesse argues that models are essential for building theories and suggesting hypotheses:

> If gases are really like collections of billiard balls, except in regard to the known negative analogy, then from our knowledge of the mechanics of billiard balls we may be able to make new predictions about the expected behavior of gases. Of course the

predictions may be wrong, but then we shall be led to conclude
that we have the wrong model.

(Hesse 1966, 9)

It is not a great leap from metaphors and analogies to fictions and
fables. Much of the work in this area is due to Nancy Cartwright. In
her classic book, *How the Laws of Physics Lie*, Cartwright introduces
her simulacrum account of explanation and makes the claim that "a
model is a work of fiction. Some properties ascribed to objects in the
model will be genuine properties of the objects modeled, but others
will be merely properties of convenience" (Cartwright 1983, 153). The
properties of convenience make mathematical theory applicable to the
objects being modeled (Bailer-Jones 2009). In addition, Cartwright
argues, in a view similar to ours, that models serve a variety of purposes,
and any particular model should be judged according to how well it
serves the purpose at hand.[4]

A more recent example comes from Godfrey-Smith (2006, 735),
who notes that "modelers often *take* themselves to be describing
imaginary biological populations, imaginary neural networks, or
imaginary economies." He defines an imaginary population as one that,
if it were real, would be a "flesh-and-blood" population. He suggests
that these imagined populations should be treated as the imagined
objects of literary fiction, such as Conan Doyle's London and Tolkien's
Middle Earth. Again, in a view similar to ours, Godfrey-Smith claims
that models are partial and provides an amusing example noting that
when most people read *Lord of the Rings*, few imagine how many toes
an orc has (2006, 735). In addition, he claims that we could describe
these fictional worlds in mathematical terms, just like an economy,
and we can easily compare them just as fiction fans might discuss the
similarities between two fictional worlds (Middle Earth and Narnia) or
the similarities between a fictional world and a real one (Middle Earth
and medieval Europe) (737).

In later work, Cartwright (1991) defends a claim that the
relationship of moral to fable is like the relationship of scientific law
to model. The argument is that fables transform the abstract into

the concrete by providing "graspable, intuitive content for abstract, symbolic judgments" (58). The moral is a symbolic claim, and the fable provides specific content. Models work in the same way, giving specific content to scientific laws, which are symbolic. Laws are true in models just as morals are true in fables. Thus, a model "fits out" a scientific law by providing a concrete example where the law holds.

Noted economist Ariel Rubinstein also sees models as fables or fairy tales (2006, 881). The difference in the accounts is that Cartwright is concerned with the abstract versus the concrete, whereas Rubinstein claims that both models and fables parallel situations in the world and both impart a lesson. For Rubinstein, a fable, like a model, abstracts from irrelevant detail and may seem unrealistic or simplistic. This lack of detail may allow us to see connections that might otherwise remain hidden. Although fables exist in a netherworld between fantasy and reality, they teach us something—a moral or a lesson—about the world, and those lessons can have significant consequences. Models, therefore, are neither of the real world nor completely divorced from it. Rubinstein's (2006, 882) conclusion is that it makes no more sense to test a model than it does to test a fable.

In a final account, Morrison and Morgan (1999b) see models as mediating instruments. That is, models stand, or mediate, between theories and the world and are partially independent of both. This partial independence arises from the ways scientists construct models. Built from bits of theory, bits of data, and a structure that may be mathematical, models comprise a "mixture of elements," including some from outside the field of inquiry (Morrison and Morgan 1999b, 14). Although models are only partially independent, they can function autonomously as instruments to aid scientists in the exploration of both theories and the world. This learning occurs not only through the construction of models (learning occurs when modeling choices are made) but also through the manipulation or use of models. The authors point to the urn model in statistics as an example of a model (in this case a thought experiment) that has taught generations of students the behavior of certain probability laws.

These accounts have a number of points in common. They all describe models as partial representations of objects of interest. They all note the limited accuracy of models. Finally, they all argue that models reflect the interests of the user either through the choice of metaphor or analogy or fable or through their construction and subsequent use. These accounts also differ in a particular way. The first four describe models as linguistic entities: metaphors, analogies, fictions, or fables. In the final account, models are more similar to tools or instruments, which is also true of our account, presented in chapter 3.

1.3 THE BROAD THEMES OF THE BOOK

Five major themes or principles can be found throughout the book: science is not what we think it is; current practice is not "philosophy-free"; models are objects; models are not tested with data, but with models of data; and theoretical models are a necessary component of explanations. These themes form the core of our book, and understanding them is essential to putting the "scientific" part of political science on a firmer foundation.

1.3.1 Science Is Not What We Think It Is

By and large, political scientists, and social scientists in general, know very little about the mechanics of the modern natural sciences. If there is one thing that philosophers of science, who go out and study the natural sciences, can teach us, it is that the practices of the natural sciences are not as we imagine them (Cartwright 1983). No one actually knows what it means for a discipline to be scientific, and any set of rules we could write down would be found to be violated routinely in fields regarded as indisputably scientific. There is no such thing as *the* Scientific Method, and most philosophers have given up the search for a single set of practices that defines one field as scientific and another as not (Laudan 1983; Caldwell 1988). Many of the features of a discipline that we think of as scientific come from nineteenth-century classical physics, which holds little relevance for modern physics and even less for the modern social sciences (Giere 1984).

The question of how to divide the scientific from the nonscientific is known as the demarcation problem, and the attempt to solve it most familiar to political scientists is Popper's (1968) falsifiability criterion, which remains a touchstone for some political scientists and some political science methodology texts such as King, Keohane, and Verba (1994). Examples abound, however, of pseudo-sciences with some falsifiable theories (e.g., astrology) and legitimate natural sciences with some nonfalsifiable theories (e.g., biology and physics) (Laudan 1983).[5] Falsifiability is simply neither a necessary nor a sufficient condition for a field to be deemed scientific.

The scientific status of political science was of great concern to modern pioneers, such as William Riker, as they sought to reshape the field. Since that time, political science has matured into a full-fledged discipline that no longer needs to defend its methods to those outside the profession (although we may still argue about those methods within the profession). The only people who still care about the scientific status of political science are political scientists motivated by a largely unnecessary academic inferiority complex. For those who remain concerned, we therefore stipulate that political science is scientific. It is an easy declaration to make given that no workable definition of "scientific" exists. The claim is essentially meaningless.

1.3.2 Current Practice Is Not "Philosophy-Free"

Thinking through the implications of a model-based science and understanding the role that models play in political science unavoidably requires some discussion of the philosophy of science. The topic is not popular among practical political scientists. The prevailing view seems to be that any discussion of the philosophy of science is a diversion and a waste of time. After all, there is real work to be done. King, Keohane, and Verba (1994)'s influential text, for example, avoids "abstract philosophical debates" (3) and "issues in the philosophy of science" (6). The subject is studiously avoided in most of Brady and

Collier (2004), with the exception of McKeown (2004), and never appears in Morton (1999).[6] One prominent political scientist has been known to state that he will turn to the philosophy of science once he has retired from doing actual political science.

This antipathy toward the philosophy of science is one part of an interesting dualism that exists in political science. The same political scientists who denigrate philosophical discussion have strong and often unyielding opinions on what Science is and how Science works. As the epigraph to this chapter suggests, these opinions neither form in a vacuum, nor are they the product of observation. King, Keohane, and Verba (1994), while eschewing philosophical debate, firmly commit themselves to a particularly old brand of positivism that has not been current in half a century, all while presenting their ideas regarding research design as being based on underlying rules of inference that exist independently of philosophy. (See Johnson [2006] for a thorough discussion of the positivist commitments made by King, Keohane, and Verba [1994].) The opinions of others are influenced by limited introductions to the works of Karl Popper, Imre Lakatos, and Thomas Kuhn, or by high school and college chemistry or physics textbooks with sidebars on the Scientific Method. In many cases, researchers no longer remember the origins of these practices and have come to believe that political science research is simply done that way. Time and again, our current methodological practices are presented as "philosophy-free." Such claims are baseless.

Research practice in political science currently revolves around theory testing. A theory is proposed, an implication is derived from it, and the implication is then tested with data. If the implication is upheld in the data, the theory is deemed confirmed. If not, the theory is deemed unconfirmed. This procedure is known as the hypothetico-deductive method, and it lies at the heart of Popper's falsificationism and statistical hypothesis testing. More importantly, the procedure is central to much current research in political science. In making this case, we cite numerous examples from the leading journals and the seminal books in the field. Hypothetico-deductivism (H-D) even permeates books on political science research, some of which mention

H-D explicitly, such as Green and Shapiro (1994) and Elster (2007), and others that do not, such as Morton (1999). Even proponents of the Empirical Implications of Theoretical Models (EITM) project such as Aldrich and Alt (2003), Granato and Scioli (2004), and Granato, Lo, and Wong (2010), who relentlessly argue for H-D, never mention it by name or discuss its origins in the field.

H-D is far from "philosophy-free"; it is the subject of a wide-ranging literature in philosophy, much of it critical. We trace the rise of H-D in our discipline, showing how a group of philosophers known as the logical positivists influenced political scientists such as Riker. Our purpose in introducing some philosophy of science is not to argue that we should be deeply engaged in philosophical debate or slavishly devoted to the latest philosophical pronouncement, but rather to illuminate the influence of old philosophies on modern social scientific practices and ask whether these procedures are justified in the context of a model-based science. It is telling that models, which are so central to modern science and political science, play almost no role in those older philosophies.

1.3.3 Models Are Objects

As noted earlier, any political scientist with a model will quickly and cheerfully tell anyone who will listen that of course his or her model is false.[7] Such a declaration, however, implies something very specific about the nature of models: that models are capable of being true or false. This way of thinking about models is a holdover from the philosophy of the mid-twentieth century when proponents of the so-called Received View argued that scientific theories comprised sentences or propositions, which can be true or false. The Received View enjoys little or no currency today outside of the social sciences, where its influence generally goes unrecognized. If there is one thing that those who think deeply about models agree on, it is that models are actually not truth-apt (Contessa 2009).

The modern approach sees models as objects; to ask whether an object is true or false is to make a category mistake. Objects are neither.

Toy airplanes, teapots, and trees are not capable of being true or false any more than models are. Thinking of models as objects is intuitive when it comes to three-dimensional models, such as the miniatures used by architects to communicate ideas to clients or Matchbox cars. It is far less intuitive to think of models as objects when it comes to the mathematical models used in the social sciences. All models, however, are representations, and representations are objects that stand in for other objects. We study one thing, the phenomenon, by studying another thing, the model. Thus, instead of studying the U.S. Congress directly, we create a model of the Congress and investigate the model. Once we are willing to view models as objects, the correct question to ask is not whether the model (object) is true or false but whether the model (object) is useful for achieving some purpose.

We go beyond arguing that models are objects; we argue that models are like particular kinds of objects—maps. We stress repeatedly that models share many of the properties of maps. Like maps, models have limited accuracy, models are partial, and most importantly, models are purpose-relative. The way to judge a map is to ask not whether it is true or false but whether it is useful for a specific purpose. The same holds for models; truth or falsity is irrelevant. The true measure of a model is usefulness, and we detail the different ways that theoretical and empirical models can be useful.

Theoretical models, we argue, can be useful in any one or more of four different roles: foundational (providing a basis for further model building or constructing a flexible and adaptive model), organizational (collecting disparate empirical generalizations, theoretical results, or set of facts under a single framework), exploratory (investigating mechanisms or motivations underlying phenomena of interest), and predictive (generating comparative statics). Empirical models are useful in one or more of three different roles: prediction (postdicting and forecasting), measurement (improving the quantification of difficult concepts), and characterization (describing data and spotting provocative associations). We argue that a fourth use of empirical models, theory testing, is the one for which they are least suited.

Though we do not insist on precisely these particular categorizations, we do insist that usefulness is the correct criterion for judging models.

1.3.4 Models Are Not Tested with Data

Political scientists often talk and write about testing their models with data. Indeed, much of the recent action in political methodology has concerned the EITM project, which focuses on the testability and testing of theoretical models. The argument is that confronting theoretical models with data brings with it a number of benefits, including more grounded theoretical models, less whimsical empirical models, and fewer irrelevant deductions.

One problem with this formulation is that theoretical models are not tested with data. Rather, theoretical models are confronted with models of data, which we also refer to as data models or empirical models. These kinds of models share all the attributes of theoretical models: they are partial, have limited accuracy, and are purpose-relative. A data model acts as a map of the relationships and dependencies within a data set.

The question now becomes how do two models—both of which are limited, partial, and purpose-relative—comment on one another? How precisely does an empirical model test a theoretical model? Why do political scientists privilege the empirical model (that which does the testing) over the theoretical model (that which is tested) when both are models?

1.3.5 Explanation

Empirical models cannot test theoretical models, and often such tests are unnecessary given the nature of theoretical models. There are instances, however, where theoretical and empirical models interact. Explanation is one of those instances. Although political science is rife with all manner of debates (e.g., rational choice versus anti-rational choice; qualitative versus quantitative), there is nearly universal agreement that explanation is an important goal.

There is less agreement about what constitutes an explanation. For many political scientists, demonstrating that x causes y amounts to an explanation. We challenge that view and argue that empirical models cannot provide explanations independently of theoretical models because empirical models provide neither arguments nor mechanisms. Explanations, therefore, must comprise either a theoretical model or a theoretical model and an empirical model.

Choosing between explanations that contain both a theoretical model and an empirical model is possible only in a relative sense. That is, using model discrimination techniques, we can say (albeit with uncertainty) that one explanation is better than another explanation. Both explanations, however, may be bad. Often, choosing between explanations is unnecessary. Seemingly rival explanations may simply be addressing different questions or addressing parts of a complex situation.

1.4 PLAN OF THE BOOK

In chapter 2, we paint a picture of where political science is at this moment in time. We do that by directly quoting from the work of top researchers in the field. The books from which we quote serve as exemplars for other faculty and, most importantly, for graduate students. We demonstrate that these books all rely on H-D. We discuss H-D in detail and show how it underlies commonly accepted parts of our methodological approach, such as falsificationism and classical hypothesis testing. After demonstrating the pervasiveness of H-D in political science, we detail the problems associated with H-D that have led many outside of the social sciences to abandon it. In particular, we show that the deductive structure of H-D prevents us from learning anything about the model that we did not already know. Finally, we trace the influence of H-D in political science to Riker's commitment to logical positivism. We argue that Riker's commitment is carried on today by two seminal methodology texts and the EITM project.

In chapter 3, we answer the question, "what is a model?" Our broad claim is that models share many of the same properties as maps; indeed, little damage is done to the concept of a model to think of models as maps. An extended discussion of maps illuminates those properties they share with models—maps are not truth-apt, maps have limited accuracy, maps are partial, and maps are purpose-relative. We then contrast the Received View of models, the view of models associated with logical positivism, with its successors, the Semantic Conception and the model-based view. Where the former is concerned with theories and truth, the latter deal with models and representation. The chapter ends with a discussion of the relationship between theories and models. Theories, on the model-based view, are simply collections or sets of models and are of minor importance when compared with models.

Chapter 4 is devoted to theoretical models, which are characterized by their reliance on deductive reasoning, their technique (e.g., social choice and game theory), and their level of abstraction. We argue that there are many ways to categorize models, but in keeping with our focus, we create a classification scheme that is consistent with usefulness and purpose. Models serve in any one or more of four different roles: foundational, organizational, exploratory, and predictive. We argue that models should be judged not by how well they predict, which is a common standard, but by how useful they are. This approach avoids the arbitrary precision of cookbook methodologies, but properly calls attention to the role of taste in choosing between theoretical models.

Empirical models are the subject of chapter 5. We begin by defining what an empirical model is and its relationship to the data. We discuss how to understand an empirical model under the model-based account. We argue that empirical models can be useful in one or more of three ways: prediction, measurement, and characterization. We pay particular attention to theory testing as the most common use of empirical models and the use to which empirical models are least suited. We demonstrate that the combination of an H-D relationship between the theoretical model and the hypothesis to be tested and an H-D relationship between the hypothesis to be tested and the data prevents model testing. This logic holds regardless of the statistical approach—falsificationist, verificationist, or Bayesian—taken. We then address the other uses of empirical modeling in part by presenting examples of such models drawn from the political science literature that eschew theory testing while remaining useful and, by most accounts, scientific.

Chapter 6 begins with a question. How do theoretical and empirical models interact? Theoretical models are not confronted with data, but with models of data, or empirical models. Theoretical models and empirical models represent different things; given that there is no testing relationship, or even a strictly logical relationship, between them, what is the nature of their interaction? We consider existing justifications for combining theoretical and empirical models and find them wanting. We argue for a new justification based on the premise that theoretical models are necessary components of explanations. We discuss two broad conceptions of explanation, the unification approach and the causal-mechanical approach, and show that political scientists make use of both. An introduction to choosing between explanations in a relative sense and whether choosing is always necessary ends the chapter.

We conclude in chapter 7 by addressing many of the criticisms that the arguments made in this book have raised.

1.5 WHAT THIS BOOK IS NOT

Although this book may be many things, there are a few that it is not. First, this book is about models in political science. It is not about building, solving, or estimating models; those skills are learned in graduate training programs. Rather, it is a book on understanding the role that models play in political science once they have been written down. Those interested in learning to construct and solve theoretical models should consult Ordeshook (1986), Kreps (1990), Fudenberg and Tirole (1991), and Gibbons (1992). Those interested in learning to construct and estimate empirical models should consult Davidson and MacKinnon (1981), Wooldridge (2002), Greene (2003), and Cameron and Trivedi (2005).

Along the same lines, our book is not a cookbook in the sense of providing recipes, which if followed precisely every time, will produce a consistently sapid outcome. In a world where *the* Scientific Method does not exist, there are simply too many different combinations of ingredients, temperatures, and cooking times (to stretch a metaphor) that can produce good work. Our book is rather one of first principles in which we help researchers think more carefully about their models and avoid making claims that are antithetical to the nature of models.

This book is also not a primer on the philosophy of science or the philosophy of economics. We draw on these disciplines selectively and discuss only a tiny fraction of the issues they raise. Those interested in broader introductions to the philosophy of science should consult Suppe (1977), Chalmers (1982), Salmon et al. (1992), and Boyd, Gasper, and Trout (1993). Hausman (1992) and Stigum (2003) are the "go-to" sources for the philosophy of economics. Those directly interested in models should look at van Fraassen (1980), Rappaport (1998), and Bailer-Jones (2009).

This book has little to say directly about qualitative research, experimental research, and computational modeling. These topics are not featured not because they are unimportant but because the conversation in political science in recent years has revolved around formal models and statistical models (mostly due to the EITM project). That being said, we see no reason the argument we make in this book should not apply to these parts of the discipline. In fact, it seems that a model-based view of science would be a particular boon to computational modelers, who are still struggling to gain acceptance within political science. There is some evidence, as we note in chapter 3, that computational modelers in political science already think in ways that are similar to our approach.

Finally, our book is not an attempt to limit what the field views as good work. We are neither opponents of rational choice, nor do we claim that theoretical and empirical models have nothing to say to one another. Whereas the definition of good work in political science has narrowed to comprising a formal model (or at least a detailed soft model) matched with an empirical model that serves as a test of the formal model, we provide a number of examples in chapters 4 and 5 of theoretical models that are useful without being tested and empirical models that are useful without having been derived from a formal model. One of our goals is to get the field to acknowledge and appreciate a wider range of scholarship as being good and useful.

The Science in Political Science

One is still exhorted—particularly in courses in methodology associated with the social and behavioral sciences—to formulate one's hypotheses clearly, to draw testable implications from them by deductively valid reasoning, and to put these implications to experimental test without fear or favor.

—Philosopher and computer scientist HENRY KYBURG, JR.

2.1 INTRODUCTION

What or where, exactly, is the science in political science? Those engaged in the practice of political science probably do not stop to ask themselves this question very often. After all, there is a lot of work to be done, and in the minds of many, this issue has long been settled: it is well understood that political science is a science.

Put on the spot, however, any political scientist worth her salt could provide a more or less coherent answer. Thinking back to the "scope and methods" course all budding social science scholars take in graduate school, the political scientist would answer that the method used by political scientists puts the "science" in political science. Students learn this lesson from three sources. The first is pioneering work in the discipline that is explicitly concerned with being scientific. The second source is books on social science methodology, such as King, Keohane, and Verba (1994) and Morton (1999), that systematize and concretize advice from the first source. The final source is those few philosophers of science—Karl Popper, Imre

Lakatos, and Thomas Kuhn—who have made their way into the political science canon.

The method is easily summarized: science comes from ruthlessly subjecting speculative theories to data (Chalmers 1982). This work is done following a script with enormous intuitive appeal matched only by its elegant simplicity. There are three steps. A theory is proposed. A prediction is derived from the theory. In the final step, the prediction is checked against the facts. If the facts deem the prediction true, the theory gains credibility. If the facts deem the prediction false, the theory loses credibility. Thus, the facts keep a check on our flights of fancy, and the end result is science.

What if we were to press deeper and ask just what it is about this three-step method—propose, derive, and test—that makes it scientific? What if we asked for the justification, the warrant, for using the method? The answer we would likely get is that this is how "real" scientists (chemists, physicists, biologists) go about their work. The problem with this answer is that it is wrong. The impression, held by many political scientists, that this method is the hallmark of true science often comes from textbooks used in high school or college science courses. It is the rare textbook, however, that accurately reflects the growth of a science. More often, textbooks take sophisticated scientific arguments and reframe them in the mold of the three-step method even when such justifications are nonsensical (Glymour 1980b). Scholars who study the history and philosophy of science have observed how "real scientists" do their work, and their conclusion is clear: science is not that simple (Cartwright 1983).

The purpose of the current chapter is threefold. First, we demonstrate that political scientists believe in and make use of the three-step method. We cite leading publications in the discipline, textbooks, and the results of a survey of journal articles. Second, we explain some of the technical aspects of the method and discuss the many reasons the method is problematic. Finally, we trace how political science became enamored of the three-step method by looking at the writings of William Riker, considered by many to be the founder of positive political theory. We also consider more recent work that perpetuates the use of the three-step method. Such work includes the Empirical Implications of Theoretical Models (EITM) project, which through its two summer institutes is responsible for training a generation of graduate students.

2.2 WHAT POLITICAL SCIENTISTS SAY THEY ARE DOING

We begin by taking a look at what top political scientists say they are doing in their own work. These explications of method are important for two reasons. First, these authors are making the implicit argument that other political scientists should follow in their methodological footsteps. As we will see, some of these scholars go so far as to identify their particular methodology as *the* Scientific Method. Second, these books are read by and taught to thousands of graduate students who learn how to do political science, in part, by emulating these books. Of course, the implicit promise that goes along with the implicit argument is that if you follow these steps, you, too, will be doing science.

After reading the many quotes we provide, some might make the argument that we interpret the authors too literally and "no one really thinks that." Whether the political scientists we quote think in the same way as they write, however, is immaterial. Even if we believed that a scholar can separate how she writes from how she thinks (and, for the record, we do not believe that), what matters are the ideas being transmitted through the work. After all, no one knows the private doubts the author might have had or whether the three-step method was followed assiduously. It is probably not infrequent that predictions are reverse engineered into a model after being found in an empirical analysis so as to comply with the three-step method. All we can judge, and all a student can learn from, is the actual written words. If an author meant something different, it is incumbent upon her to write down exactly what she did mean.

We begin with one of the touchstones of modern political science, John Zaller's (1992) *The Nature and Origins of Mass Opinion*, in which the author argues that mass public opinion is determined by exposure to the discourse of elites. Zaller writes down a model that accounts both for how citizens learn political information and how they turn that information into public opinion. The "Receive-Accept-Sample" model comprises four axioms: reception (those who cognitively engage with an issue are more likely to receive political messages), resistance (people are resistant to arguments that are inconsistent with their political predispositions), accessibility (recent considerations are more accessible than older considerations), and response (opinion comes from averaging across easily accessible considerations). Zaller uses these four axioms to "explore and explain numerous aspects of mass opinion" (51). Although he argues that his model is not "perfectly true" (42), he proceeds to test it in the rest of the book. Specifically, he writes,

> The method of the book, then, is to develop the deductive implications of the four basic axioms for a given, highly specific set of conditions; review evidence indicating whether or not these implications are empirically correct; and present new evidence as necessary and possible to resolve outstanding empirical questions.
>
> (Zaller 1992, 51)

The scientific part of the analysis takes a clearly recognizable form. The first step is to write down the model, which in this case comprises the four axioms. The second step is to derive deductive implications, or predictions, from the model. The third step is to test the model by checking these implications against the data. Thus, Zaller is proposing and arguing for the three-step method: propose, derive, and test. Much of the book is a discussion of how difficult it is for the author to test this particular model.

Zaller is not alone, of course. In *Information and Legislative Organization*, Keith Krehbiel argues that informational concerns are key to understanding how legislatures are organized. Specifically, he argues that the structure of committees influences whether committee members gather information about the consequences of legislation and faithfully transmit that data to the entire legislature. Toward the start of the book, Krehbiel describes his methodology, which bears more than a passing similarity to Zaller's:

> To reap the benefits of a joint theoretical-empirical approach, the remainder of this study seeks to conform with orthodox tenets of positive social science. Postulates are empirically motivated. Theoretical assumptions are explicit and precise. Theoretical results follow logically from the assumptions. Empirical predictions are extracted from theoretical results. And empirical predictions are refutable. That is, key concepts can be measured, measures are amenable to data analysis, and data analysis makes it possible to support or refute the theories in question.
>
> (Krehbiel 1991, 15)

It is easy to see that Krehbiel's method is, in its essentials, the same as Zaller's. Implications (predictions) are deductively (logically) derived from a model and then tested. Once again, this is the three-step method. Krehbiel goes beyond Zaller, however, in claiming that the method constitutes the "orthodox tenets of positive political science." We explore how these "orthodox tenets" came to be later in the chapter.

Comparative politics scholars and international relations scholars preach the same methodological sermon. In *War and Reason*, Bruce Bueno de Mesquita and David Lalman develop and test the international interaction game through which they hope to explain many of the theoretical puzzles facing international relations scholars. In their disquisition on modeling, Bueno de Mesquita and Lalman (1992, 22) write, "The science of modeling depends on the ability to extract testable, falsifiable relationships among variables that follow in a logically coherent fashion, so that the connection between the model's structure and its empirical implications is clear and consistent." In summarizing their results, the authors write,

> We have suggested solutions to each of these and many other theoretical or empirical puzzles. In virtually every case the

proposed solution has satisfied the following formula: first the solution has been formally deduced and proved in the context of our theory, then the hypothesized solution has been submitted to empirical scrutiny through the analysis of the historical record. We have endeavored to be explicit about the expectations in our empirical tests so that the conditions for falsification are clear.

(Bueno de Mesquita and Lalman 1992, 270)

This quote contains an explicit mention of falsificationism, which is one name given to the three-step method. The other name is hypothetico-deductivism (H-D), and we demonstrate the connection between the two later in the chapter. Despite the use of a different term, Bueno de Mesquita and Lalman describe the same method used by Zaller and Krehbiel.

The three-step method is also easily found in comparative politics, typically regarded as the least technical of the traditional political science subfields (excluding political philosophy). Robert Bates (2008, 8–9) makes the explicit claim that employing the three-step method sets his work on state failure apart:

In this work, I proceed in a different fashion. I start by first capturing the logic that gives rise to political order. While I, too, test hypotheses about the origins of disorder, I derive these hypotheses from a theory. By adopting a more deductive approach, I depart from the work of my predecessors.

In her treatise on methods and research design in comparative politics, Geddes (2003, 87) claims that progress on explaining outcomes such as democratization can be made using the three-step method: "Coherent deductive arguments can be devised to explain constituent processes, and hypotheses derived from the arguments can be tested." She goes on to write that "an argument from which an implication has been tested on evidence from a large number of cases is more likely to prove of lasting value than an untested argument induced from a handful of cases."

Some critics might suggest that quoting leading scholars in political science is anecdotal or perhaps that books are somehow systematically different from peer-reviewed journal articles through which most political science findings are communicated. Clarke and Primo (2007) address this claim by reporting the results of a survey of the three leading generalist journals in political science: *American Political Science Review, American Journal of Political Science,* and *Journal of Politics.* Of the 738 articles published in these journals between 2001 and 2005, we randomly sampled 10 percent, or 74 articles. Using very conservative coding rules, we identified nearly half of the articles (46 percent) as using or promoting the three-step method.[1] Far from being rare, the three-step method is practiced in all subfields, with the exception of political philosophy; as the quotes suggest, it is often seen as the gold standard of political science research.

A third area, after substantive books and journal articles, where we can find the three-step method is in undergraduate textbooks written by practicing political scientists. As the connection between what political scientists think and what ends up in textbooks is more tenuous, we confine ourselves to a single example, Clark, Golder, and Golder's (2008) *Principles of Comparative Politics,* with an understanding that many others could have been chosen. After noting that there is no scientific method that is clearly written down and followed by all scientists, Clark, Golder, and Golder argue that it is possible to characterize the basic features of such a method in five steps. Step one is to "observe the world and come up with a question or puzzle" (42). Step two is to "come up with a theory or model to explain" the puzzle (43). Step three is to deduce implications from the model, and step four is to "examine whether the implications of the model are consistent with observation" (45). In step five, "if we observe the implications deduced from our theory, we simply say that our theory has been corroborated" (46). Although Clark, Golder, and Golder have stretched it to five steps, the three-step method we describe forms the core of their approach.

We have quoted just a handful of top scholars, conducted a limited survey, and looked at a modern political science textbook. We could have quoted from many more scholars from all areas of the discipline. We could have expanded our survey, and we could have quoted from more textbooks. The results would be the same. Political science, it seems, has settled on a "Scientific Method." The goal for the remainder of this chapter is to look carefully at this method, assess what is actually scientific about it, and finally, examine how the method came to dominate political science.

2.3 HYPOTHETICO-DEDUCTIVISM

All the scholars just discussed write about the same method, which we have been referring to as propose, derive, and test. The technical name for this method is hypothetico-deductivism (H-D), and we shall use that name throughout the rest of the book.

The H-D model of science works in the following way:

- a hypothesis H is set up for testing or examination;
- an observation sentence O is deduced from H and its attendant theoretical background statements, boundary conditions, etc.;
- to test the hypothesis, we set up an experiment or an examination of the world and observe either O or $\sim O$.

(Kyburg 1988, 65)

If we conclude that the observation sentence, O, is not true in the world, then we have refuted H. If we conclude that the observation sentence, O, is true in the world, then we have confirmed H or, at the very least, failed to refute it. Replace hypothesis, H, in the foregoing, with theory, T, and replace observation statement, O, with hypothesis, H, and we have the method described by Krehbiel (1991), Zaller (1992), Bueno de Mesquita and Lalman (1992), Geddes (2003), Bates (2008), and Clark, Golder, and Golder (2008). That is,

- a theory T is set up for testing;
- a hypothesis H is deduced from T and its attendant background statements, boundary conditions, etc.;
- to test the theory, we set up an experiment or an examination of the world and observe either H or $\sim H$.

Thus, we can describe the H-D model of science in the following shorthand: "Theory implies prediction (basic sentence, or observation sentence); if prediction is false, theory is falsified; if sufficiently many predictions are true, theory is confirmed" (Putnam 1991, 123).[2] A philosopher of economics describes the method this way:

> Reduced to its bare bones, this method (H-D) consists of the following four steps:
>
> 1. *Formulate* some hypothesis or theory H.
> 2. *Deduce* some "prediction" or observable claim, P, from H conjoined with a variety of other statements. These other statements will include descriptions of initial conditions, other theories, and *ceteris paribus* ("other things being equal") clauses.
> 3. *Test P.* (One tests H only indirectly by means of the H-D method.) Testing may involve complicated experimentation or simple observation.
> 4. *Judge* whether H is confirmed or disconfirmed depending on the nature of P and whether P turned out to be true or false.
>
> (Hausman 1992, 304)

Regardless of how many steps it takes—three for Putnam (1991), four for Hausman (1992), and five for Clark, Golder, and Golder (2008)—the method described is the same. One reason that political scientists are so comfortable with the H-D method, aside from its intuitive appeal, is that its influence in the discipline extends beyond theory testing. H-D is so engrained in our collective thinking that we often forget that it underlies positions and procedures we take for granted. Falsificationism, for example, is seen as the *sine qua non* element of science by many political scientists, and falsificationism is a version of H-D (Putnam 1991). Classical hypothesis testing, which is used routinely by most quantitative political scientists, is also based on H-D in a fundamental way. We explore each in turn.

Falsification is most closely associated with the work of philosopher Karl Popper, who was trying to solve what philosophers call the problem of demarcation, or distinguishing science from nonscience. According to Popper, what distinguishes the science of astronomy from the nonscience of astrology, and the science of chemistry from the nonscience of Freud, is the criterion of falsifiability. Scientific theories are falsifiable, and nonscientific theories are not. To be falsifiable means that "there exists a logically possible observation statement or set of observations statements that are inconsistent with it, that is, which, if established as true, would falsify the hypothesis" (Chalmers 1982, 40).

It is not, however, just Popper's proposed solution to the demarcation problem that interests us; it is also his proposed solution to Hume's problem of induction. Hume's concern was the justification of claims based on experience; that is, how to justify the conclusion that X is a Y based on all previously observed X's being Y's. Justifying induction requires justifying the assumption that underlies all inductive conclusions, namely, that the future will be like the past. Without this assumption, there is no such thing as induction; justifying the assumption, then, is vitally important. There are two possible avenues for justifying such a premise (Chalmers 1982). One is an appeal to logic. Consider the following inductive argument:

I was not hit by a bus three days ago.
I was not hit by a bus two days ago.
I was not hit by a bus yesterday.

I will not be hit by a bus tomorrow.

The problem with this inductive argument is that it is not logically valid.[3] The appeal to logic thus fails. The other possible avenue for justifying induction is to make an inductive argument:

Induction worked at time t.
Induction worked at time $t + 1$, etc.

_____

Induction always works.

Of course, this logic is circular; induction is being used to justify induction. Justification thus fails.

Popper argued that falsificationism is the remedy for the problem of induction. Although it is impossible to prove that a claim is true with a finite number of observations, it is possible to prove a claim is false with a single observation. Thus, although we cannot prove that the claim "all swans are white" is true without having observed all swans, we can disprove the claim by observing a single black swan. Science, Popper felt, should work the same way. Scientists should propose a conjecture, the bolder and more falsifiable the better, and then ruthlessly try to prove that it is false. Science then proceeds through a series of conjectures and refutations.

On its face, it would seem that falsificationism has little in common with H-D. The latter concerns gathering positive evidence for a claim, and the former concerns trying to prove a claim false. The connection between falsificationism and H-D is the deductive link between theory and hypothesis. At the heart of falsificationism concerns lies a logically valid deductive argument called *modus tollens* (Kyburg 1988, 62).[4] The form of the argument is simple:

If A is true then B is true $(A \rightarrow B)$,
if B is not true $(\neg B)$,
then it can be concluded that A is not true $(\neg A)$.

In purely symbolic terms, the argument is $A \rightarrow B, \neg B \vdash \neg A$, which reads "if A then B, not B, therefore not A." Examples are easy to come by. If an animal is a mammal, then it breathes air. The animal does not breathe air, therefore it is not a mammal. If we replace A with T for theory and B with H for hypothesis, we have falsificationism. If the theory is true (T) then the hypothesis holds (H); if the hypothesis does not hold $(\neg H)$, then it can be concluded that the theory is not true $(\neg T)$, or $T \rightarrow H, \neg H \vdash \neg T$.

Falsificationists differ from other practitioners of H-D in that they claim that nothing can be learned from a confirming instance. That is, they assert that concluding a theory is true based on a true hypothesis is a logical fallacy. They do not accept arguments of the form,

If the theory is true (T) then the hypothesis holds (H),

if the hypothesis holds (H),

then it can be concluded that the theory is true (T),

because such arguments are not logically valid. The name of this logical fallacy, symbolically $T \rightarrow H, H \vdash T$, is *affirming the consequent*. Continuing our example, if an animal is a mammal, then it breathes air. The animal breathes air, therefore it is a mammal. Such an argument is clearly not valid because reptiles breathe air, and reptiles are not mammals.

Given that theories cannot be proved true, how a theory becomes accepted according to falsificationists remains a question. Popper's answer is that a "degree" of confirmation or corroboration is awarded to theories that survive numerous difficult falsification attempts. Here lies the famous "whiff of induction." The more tests of increasing difficulty a theory survives, the more we should come to believe it, according to Popper. Falsificationism, in this sense, is even closer to H-D than is apparent at first glance.

Classical hypothesis testing is another H-D procedure that political scientists often take for granted. Although quantitatively oriented researchers perform such hypothesis tests nearly every day in the normal course of doing their work, few realize that the procedure takes the form of a *modus tollens* argument (Kyburg 1988; Clarke 2007a).

Explaining how hypothesis tests came to have this form requires some background knowledge on the problem of significance testing. Statistical hypotheses cannot be refuted in any strict sense. Consider the statistical hypothesis that the probability of observing heads when flipping a fair coin is one-half. If we flip a coin twenty times, there is no outcome of the experiment that is inconsistent with the hypothesis that the coin is fair. Observing twenty heads in twenty tosses is unlikely, but not impossible. The problem of how to falsify statistical hypotheses has been around at least since Cournot, and the significance test was Fisher's solution (Howson and Urbach 1993, 171). The idea is that a hypothesis should be rejected when the data (the evidence) are relatively unlikely to have occurred under the assumption that the hypothesis is true.[5]

In practice, the hypothesis under consideration implies a value of a test statistic (in political science this value is often zero), which can also be expressed as a probability. If the sample statistic (or probability) is sufficiently far enough away from the value of the test statistic implied by the null hypothesis, and thus has a low probability of occurring under the null, the hypothesis is rejected. Consider the following political science example borrowed from Freedman, Pisani, and Purves (1998, 541):

> In a certain town, there are about one million eligible voters. A simple random sample of size 10,000 was chosen, to study the relationship between sex and participation in the last election. The results:

	Men	Women
Voted	2,792	3,591
Didn't vote	1,486	2,131

The null hypothesis that participation and gender are independent of one another implies that the value of the χ^2 statistic should be about 1 (the degree of freedom), give or take about the standard error or $\sqrt{2}$ (the variance is twice the degrees of freedom, so the standard error is the square root of twice the degrees of freedom). The observed test statistic is 6.55, which gives a probability of 0.01. Using the 5 percent convention, then, we would reject the null hypothesis of independence.

We can see the deductive structure of the test just performed if we express it in symbols. The null hypothesis of independence, H_0, implies that the probability of observing the data given the assumption that the null is true, $P(y|H_0)$, is large. The actual probability of observing the data given the assumption that the null is true, $P(y|H_0)$, is small (0.01). Thus, we reject the null hypothesis, $\neg H_0$. The test, written compactly in logical form, is

$$\left. \begin{array}{ll} (1) \ H_0 \rightarrow P(y|H_0) & \text{is large,} \\ (2) \qquad\quad P(y|H_0) & \text{is small} \end{array} \right\} \vdash \neg H_0,$$

which reads, "if H_0 then $P(y|H_0)$ is large, $P(y|H_0)$ is small, therefore not H_0." This structure is precisely that of *modus tollens*, $A \rightarrow B$, $\neg B \vdash \neg A$, with the exception that it is not a logically valid argument due to the use of probabilities (if the premises are true, the conclusion is not necessarily true). Nonetheless, we arrive at a conclusion through the process of deducing a consequence from a hypothesis and testing it.

We revisit the issue of H-D and classical hypothesis testing in chapter 5, but the important points for now are how thoroughly H-D is intertwined in our professional lives and why that is problematic.

2.4 PROBLEMS WITH H-D

On its face, H-D appears hard to argue with. After all, nothing could be more straightforward than proposing a theory, deriving a prediction or implication from it, and testing the prediction. Political science, however, has adopted H-D rather uncritically. It is unclear precisely what is scientific about the use of H-D. Moreover, it is unclear why political scientists should believe that use of the H-D method will result in scientific progress. The spread of the falsificationist strain of H-D seems to stem not from its successes but from its simplicity:

> There seem to be several reasons for his [Popper's] impact on economic methodology. One appears to be the common perception that Popper's philosophy is relatively straightforward and easy to apply; his prose is clear and unpretentious, and the falsificationist program seems to offer a relatively simple demarcation criterion as well as a set of easily implemented methodological rules for the proper conduct of scientific inquiry (i.e., it makes good 3" x 5" card philosophy of science).
>
> (Hands 2001, 276)

Another reason for H-D's ubiquity stems from the fact that we make use of this kind of reasoning every day in our own lives. A political scientist named Bob might think the following: "if I am on time for the bus, I will see a group of people waiting at the corner. If I do not see anyone waiting at the corner, I conclude that I am not on time for the bus." The deductive model of reasoning just comes naturally. The problem, however, is that once we begin to push past the intuitive appeal of the H-D model, its straightforwardness collapses. Take the bus example. You probably noted when you read it that Bob's conclusion was not necessarily correct. Perhaps Bob was not late for the bus at all, but rather, it was a holiday, and his usual mass transportation buddies did not have to go to work and therefore were not waiting for the bus. Perhaps the bus route changed the night before, and Bob's companions were waiting on a different corner. Perhaps the bus route had changed because it was a holiday. The list of possible explanations is nearly infinite.

Our commuter faces other problems as well. Bob relied on his eyes to transmit accurately the data and on his brain to interpret the data correspondingly. We cannot always trust these organs, of course. Perhaps a fall the night before had altered Bob's visual perception, and he failed to see the people waiting on the corner. A misfiring synapse in the brain could have the same effect. So the H-D model is not as foolproof as we might imagine, and our example is simple. When we get to actual science, these problems multiply.

A reader may object at this point that Bob's original claim—if I am on time for the bus, I will see a group of people waiting at the corner—might hold *ceteris paribus*. What such a claim means, though, is unclear. Note that Bob muttering *ceteris paribus* to himself as he approaches the bus stop does him no good whatsoever. Invoking *ceteris paribus* does not help explain why no one is waiting at the bus stop, and it does nothing to help sort through the myriad possible explanations. In the context of H-D, *ceteris paribus* claims are used by researchers mostly to render claims immune from falsification.

These problems with the H-D approach, as well as others, are well known. By 1980, attempts to justify the supposedly intuitive H-D model had become so complex that one leading philosopher titled an article "Hypothetico-Deductivism Is Hopeless" (Glymour 1980a), and another was left to argue rather impotently about H-D's ineffable rightness (Grimes 1990). What could be so wrong with such an intuitive procedure? We begin with two shortcomings that are particularly relevant to political scientists: the truth-preserving nature of deductions and the fact that data cannot speak for themselves.

2.4.1 Deductions Are Truth-Preserving

First, what can one learn about the truth of a model from testing an implication of that model? The answer is "nothing that we did not know before." The key to this result is understanding the nature of a valid deduction. Consider the following valid argument: $A \rightarrow B, A \vdash B$, which reads, "if A then B, A, therefore B." What is true of this argument and all deductive arguments is that if the premises are true, then the conclusion must be true. Deductions are truth-preserving. Thus, if $A \rightarrow B$ and A are true, then the conclusion B must be true. In the context of our example, if the premises, "if I am on time then I will see other riders at the corner," and "I am on time" are true, then the conclusion, "I see other riders at the corner" must be true. *Because deductive arguments are truth-preserving, testing conclusions arrived at deductively is unnecessary and redundant.* Of course, one might argue that deductions should be tested to ensure that the deductions were made correctly (Morton 1999, 102). The results of such tests, however, cannot distinguish between deductions that were arrived at incorrectly due to mistakes in logic and deductions that are wrong because the premises are wrong. The observational consequences—a false prediction—are the same.

To amplify that last point, if the assumptions of a model are false, then we do not know anything about the conclusions that are deduced from the model. It is not true to state that if the assumptions of a model are false, then the deduced implications of the model must be false. We simply do not know in such a case because deductive arguments are not falsity-preserving. Consider again the valid argument: $A \to B$, $A \vdash B$. If the second premise A is not true, then we cannot conclude that B is true. Furthermore, we cannot even conclude that B is false. If the premise "I am on time" is false, there may or may not be public transportation riders waiting at the corner. When at least one premise of a deductive argument is false, the conclusion may be either true or false because there is no longer any connection between the premises and the conclusion.[6]

Using what we have learned about deductions—that they are truth-preserving but not falsity-preserving—we can write down the two possible states of the world for any deductive argument: one where both the assumptions and the predictions are true, and one where the assumptions are false. These states of the world are depicted in table 2.1. The assumptions of a deductive theory are either true or false. If the assumptions of the theory are true, then the

Table 2.1. Possible States of the World

	Cases	
	(1)	(2)
Assumptions	True	False
Predictions	True	True or False
Connection between model and truth of prediction	Logical necessicity	None
Informativeness of data analysis for "truth" of model	Uninformative	Uninformative

predictions deductively derived from the theory must be true due to the truth-preserving nature of deduction. If the assumptions are false, then the predictions deductively derived from the theory may be true or false because there is no longer any necessary connection between the theory and the truth of the deduced prediction. What this means is that false predictions derived from theories with false assumptions cannot inform us about the truth of the theory because the deduced predictions are not connected in any necessary way to the theory.

Because political scientists never know the true state of the world, one could argue that false predictions always indicate false assumptions. The reasoning is straightforward: as table 2.1 indicates, false predictions can only come from false premises. If the argument is supposed to be $A \rightarrow B$, $A \vdash B$, a finding of not B ($\neg B$) must indicate that at least one of the two premises is false. This conclusion would be a reasonable one to draw except for the fact that *we already knew that*. Political scientists are well aware that most of the assumptions routinely used in the discipline are false. Examples include actor rationality (Doron and Sened 2001), states as unitary actors (Fearon 1995), and unicameralism (Krehbiel 1991), all of which are false and are known to be false. Because we began with a false assumption, there is nothing to be learned about the model from a prediction that turns out to be false.

A common response to this argument is that although the assumptions used by political scientists are strictly false, they are "close enough" or "near approximations" or "true enough." How close is close, though? Strictly speaking, the truth-preserving properties of a deductive model do not hold when the premises hold only approximately. There are instances in the natural sciences where the rounding of constants has no effect on deductive implications, but the assumptions used in political science are not of this type.[7] Making such an argument would necessitate use of a metric to determine the amount of the rounding. No such metric exists. It is not difficult to imagine, though, that many of our more controversial assumptions could never be considered "true enough."

Testing a prediction deductively derived from a model cannot help us learn about the model itself. A true prediction cannot tell us that the model is true, and a false prediction cannot tell us something that we already know. Testing predictions, however, is not the only way that models may be tested. Morton (1999, 161) argues that models can also be evaluated by testing their assumptions. Given the deductive (truth-preserving) nature of most models used in political science, this approach seems intuitively more reasonable than testing implications. Unfortunately, the problem with testing assumptions is very similar to the problem of "discovering" false premises. Generally, we already know that many, if not all, of our assumptions are false.

2.4.2 Data Can't Speak for Themselves

The second shortcoming concerns how we go about testing a prediction. Recall our shorthand for the H-D model of science: "Theory implies prediction (basic sentence, or observation sentence); if prediction is false, theory is falsified; if sufficiently many predictions are true, theory is confirmed" (Putnam 1991, 123). Note that little is said regarding *how* to tell whether a prediction is true or false. This lacuna exists because it was assumed that determining the truth value of a basic sentence or observation sentence was straightforward. Using just our senses, if they are to be trusted, we can tell if a group of people are waiting on a corner. Things in political science are not so simple.

Rarely in political science can the truth value of a deduced prediction be determined simply with the senses. Instead, complicated statistical equations that depend on their own sets of assumptions are required. Scholars who claim that they are letting the data speak for themselves are mistaken. Data cannot speak for themselves; some organization of the data or some interpretation of the data must take place. In political science, that almost always means an empirical model. What follows is one of the major themes of the book. Theories or models are never tested with data; they are tested with *models of data*. Theories or models are tested with imperfect empirical models. How are those empirical models tested? A good empirical model is generally thought of as one in which the "coefficients take on the expected signs." That is, based on a theoretical model, a researcher has *a priori* beliefs regarding the expected direction of coefficient effects. The empirical model is built in part to satisfy those beliefs. Thus, the data model tests the theoretical model, and the theoretical model provides grounds for accepting the data model. The resulting circularity leads nowhere.

Consider the observation sentence "Democracies do not fight one another." It would seem a relatively simply matter to identify the population of democracies and determine whether any had waged war against another member of the population. As we all know, of course, determining the truth value of this statement is quite difficult. For starters, one has to determine what a democracy is (Dahl 1971). One also must determine what a war is (Wright 1942; Singer and Small 1972). Then, because we lack experimental control, the variables *democracy* and *war* have to be embedded in a statistical model where other sources of variation are held constant. These additional concepts must be identified and then measured. We must choose the correct functional form or try to interpret the more limited information obtained from a nonparametric approach. Empirical or data models are the subject of chapter 5; suffice it to say here that determining the truth value of a prediction is often quite difficult.

It is possible that the intuitive appeal of the H-D method outweighs the shortcomings we have been discussing. Before we decide on H-D as *the* Scientific Method for political science, we discuss additional problems with the account.

2.4.3 Other Problems with H-D

The shortcomings of the H-D approach are myriad, and we only mention a few (for a full accounting, see Glymour 1980b). These problems go beyond the merely philosophical because they concern the relation of evidence to theory (Hausman 1994).

Consider, for example, the problem referred to as "the paradox of the ravens" (Hempel 1945). The paradox arises from the realization that the statement "all ravens are black" is logically equivalent to the statement "whatever is not black is not a raven." Thus, whatever evidence confirms one statement should also confirm the other statement. The problem, of course, is that the observation of a yellow pencil confirms the statement "whatever is not black is not a raven" and thus confirms the statement's equivalent "all ravens are black." The lazy investigator, therefore, need only look around his office—presumably free of ravens—to confirm that "all ravens are black."

Though the canonical example seems far removed from political science, the paradox does have implications for research. Seawright (2002), for example, argues that cases characterized by neither village autonomy nor social revolution should count as confirmatory evidence for the claim that village autonomy is a necessary condition for social revolution. By considering these cases, Seawright is able to find additional evidence for his hypothesis. Making use of these additional cases is equivalent to observing "yellow pencils" to demonstrate that "all ravens are black." The equivalence between this case and the raven paradox is discussed by Clarke (2002).

Another shortcoming of the H-D approach is the Quine-Duhem problem, which arises from the observation that no theory or hypothesis is tested in isolation. Testable predictions are derived from the hypothesis in question, supportive hypotheses, and *ceteris paribus* conditions. Therefore, it is impossible to falsify a theory or hypothesis because we cannot be sure whether the main hypothesis, one or more auxiliary hypotheses, a *ceteris paribus* clause, or a boundary condition is false. A particularly clear example comes from the international relations literature. Huth, Gelpi, and Bennett (1993) test structural realism on the population of great power extended and direct immediate deterrence encounters from 1816 to 1984. To generate testable predictions, Huth et al. combine structural realism with prospect theory (Kahneman and Tversky 1979). Although the authors claim to falsify structural realism, it is unclear whether structural realism or prospect theory or the way the two are combined caused the ill fit to the data. In addition, any number of auxiliary hypotheses concerning measurement, identification, *ceteris paribus* clauses, the functional form, or the error term could be responsible for the refutation. Where to lay the blame is unclear.[8]

"Underdetermination" refers to the logical truth that for any finite collection of evidence, there are infinitely many inconsistent hypotheses entailing that evidence. Thus, confirming that an observation sentence is true in the world does not confirm the hypothesis. To revisit our previous example, the hypotheses "the bus has already gone" and "today is a holiday" have exactly the same empirical implication: the bus does not show up. That the H-D approach cannot tell the hypotheses apart is a problem. The tacking problem or the problem of irrelevant conjunction is closely related. If some evidence confirms a hypothesis, then that evidence also confirms the conjunction of the original hypothesis with any other hypothesis, whether or not that hypothesis is relevant.

Other shortcomings of the H-D approach include the problem of nondeductive predictions and Nelson Goodman's (1979) grue paradox. The problem of nondeductive prediction refers to the fact that most hypotheses in science are statistical and thus not deductive. The grue paradox refers to the problem that all observed green emeralds confirm the statement "all emeralds are grue," where *grue* is defined as observed before A.D. 2030 and green and observed after A.D. 2030 and blue. Of course, until 2030, we can have no idea whether the second part of the claim is true. All observed green emeralds confirm the statement nonetheless.

2.5 HOW WE GOT HERE

2.5.1 Logical Positivism

To understand how H-D gained its hold in political science, we need to understand how a group of philosophers known as logical positivists thought about scientific theories and scientific explanation. We discuss these topics at greater length elsewhere (chapters 3 and 6, respectively), but a brief introduction here will prove useful. Those seeking a more detailed account of the history, tenets, and collapse of logical positivism should consult the citations in chapter 1.

Logical positivism is the philosophy associated with the famous Vienna Circle, a set of scholars who gathered in, obviously enough, Vienna, after World War I. The group included Moritz Schlick, Rudolph Carnap, Herbert Feigl, Hans Hahn, and Otto Neurath, among others (Hands 2001, 72–73). The group contended that only two kinds of knowledge exist: the analytical *a priori* and the synthetic *a posteriori* (Hausman 1992, 302). Analytic statements are sentences that are logically true. The canonical example is the sentence "All bachelors are unmarried." "One plus one equals two" is another. Synthetic statements are neither logically true nor logically false (Sellars 1956). "All bachelors are happy" and "all swans are white" are examples. An *a priori* statement is a proposition whose justification does not depend on empirical confirmation. An *a posteriori* statement is a proposition whose justification does depend on empirical confirmation. The two kinds of knowledge the logical positivists believed in, then, were logical truths and empirically verified claims about the world. To be meaningful, a statement must either be logically true or can be (in principle) proven true (or false) by experience. This assertion is known as the verifiability principle. Thus, the meaning of a statement is its method of verification; that is, the meaning of a statement is only known if the conditions under which the statement is true or false is known. The logical positivists denied the existence of synthetic *a priori* statements, or claims about the world that are neither logically true nor empirically verified.[9] Statements regarding religion, ethics, and metaphysics were rejected as meaningless.

The views of the logical positivists were particularly influential in the areas of scientific theories and scientific explanation.[10] We consider each in turn.

A scientific theory, according to the logical positivists, is a set of sentences in first-order predicate logic. Three kinds of terms comprise the axiomatization: logical and mathematical terms, theoretical terms, and observation terms. Correspondence rules provide explicit definitions that connect the theoretical terms of the theory with the

$$L_1, L_2, \ldots, L_n$$
$$C_1, C_2, \ldots, C_m$$
$$\left. \right\} \quad \text{Explanans}$$

$$E \quad \} \quad \text{Explanandum}$$

Figure 2.1 The Deductive-Nomological Model
of Explanation

observational terms. The correspondence rules render the theoretical
axioms in the theory synthetic and therefore meaningful.

A scientific explanation, according to the logical positivists, consists
of a logically valid argument where the event to be explained (called the
explanandum) deductively follows from the premises of the argument
(called the *explanans*), which consist of general laws and antecedent
conditions. This mode of explanation is variously referred to as
the covering law model of explanation (because the laws *cover* the
occurrence of the event) or the deductive-nomological model of
explanation.[11] The model is depicted in figure 2.1 where the L_i are
general laws, the C_j are initial conditions, the solid line stands for a
logical deduction, and E is the event to be explained.

The connection between H-D and the deductive-nomological
model of explanation lies in their deductive structures. The symmetry
thesis of logical positivism states that the deductive form of scientific
explanation is precisely the same as the relationship between theory
and data (Hands 2001). That is, to explain a phenomenon is to be able
to predict it deductively from a theory.

The reason for our excursion into how the logical positivists thought
about scientific explanation is that William Riker, perhaps the leading
proponent of "scientific" political science, advocated for precisely the
same thing. Riker, well versed in the philosophy of science of his
day, cited a number of leading philosophers in his work—Braithwaite,
Nagel, Hempel, Scheffler, and Popper, among others (Riker 1977,
13)—and even published two philosophy of science articles himself
(Riker 1957, 1958).

Clearly enamored of the hard sciences (as filtered through the logical positivists), Riker wrote that the intellectual edifice of the physical sciences is "the most impressive achievement of the human psyche in this or any other age" (Riker 1962, 3). He believed that the success of the hard sciences was due to the relationship between theory and predictions. "Generalizations within each science are *related* because they are deduced from one set of axioms, which, though revised from time to time, are nevertheless a coherent theoretical model of motion" (Riker 1962, 3). He goes on to argue, in a pre-Popperian vein, that "Generalizations are *verified* because, drawn as they are from a carefully constructed and precise theory, they have themselves been stated in a way that admits of verification by experiment, observation, and prediction" (Riker 1962, 4). In a later piece, he argued even more explicitly that "To explain an event is to subsume it under a covering law that, in turn, is encased in a theory" (Riker 1990, 167).

Riker's commitment to H-D and logical positivism survives in the work of political scientists today. In the next sections, we explore the hypothetico-deductivism in two seminal political science texts that deal with the connection between theory and data: Green and Shapiro's (1994) *Pathologies of Rational Choice Theory* and Morton's (1999) *Methods and Models*. Although the latter advocates for rational choice and the former does not, both are strong advocates for H-D. In addition, we address the H-D commitments of the EITM project, which plays an increasingly important role in training today's graduate students.

2.5.2 *Pathologies of Rational Choice Theory*

In their widely cited book, Donald Green and Ian Shapiro (1994) address what they see as the methodological pathologies of rational choice theory. What is interesting about the book, from our point of view, is how the criticisms the authors level at rational choice theorists clearly define how Green and Shapiro view the practice of science . . . and that view is H-D.

The pathologies Green and Shapiro discuss include post hoc theory development (retroduction, or establishing "the proposition that it is not impossible that some rational choice hypothesis might be true" [35]), slippery and vaguely operationalized predictions (arguments claiming that a successful prediction was "thwarted by an offsetting tendency or temporary aberration" [40] or that an approximation holds), searching for confirming evidence (cherry-picking evidence to support a claim), projecting evidence from theory (assuming data to be empirically verified), and arbitrary domain restriction (restricting the application of a theory to a domain where it appears to work). In discussing these so-called pathologies, Green and Shapiro make perfectly clear that they ascribe to the Popperian version of H-D (i.e., falsificationism).

For example, in their discussion of post hoc theory development, Green and Shapiro (1994, 36) write,

> rational choice theorists seldom set forth a clear statement of what datum or data, if observed, would warrant rejection of the particular hypotheses they set forth or, more generally, their conviction that politics flows from the maximizing behavior of rational actors.

Clearly, Green and Shapiro see falsificationism as the center of the "enterprise of empirical testing" (1994, 36).

If there were some doubt about their position, Green and Shapiro erase it when writing about slippery and vaguely operationalized predictions. Without qualification, they write, "To test a theory, one needs to know in advance what the theory predicts" (38). They continue that "those who seek to derive testable propositions from rational choice models frequently find, moreover, that these theories are constructed in ways that insulate them against untoward encounters with evidence" (38). When discussing vaguely operationalized predictions, Green and Shapiro are not concerned with whether testing predictions makes sense but with what *kinds* of predictions—point predictions or marginal predictions—should be tested.

Finally, Green and Shapiro (1994, 42) argue that "it is the structured search for disconfirming evidence that is essential to scientific testing." This point bolsters our contention that they believe in H-D, but only of the falsificationist kind. So although Green and Shapiro do not consider themselves "naïve falsificationists" (180), they argue for testing models by disconfirming predictions. Green and Shapiro, therefore, go beyond seeing "empirical performance as the sole criterion of good scientific practice" and advocate for the falsificationist version of H-D (Johnson 1996, 80).

Many rational choice theorists see model evaluation in precisely the same terms as Green and Shapiro do. The quote from Krehbiel earlier in the chapter attests to this fact. When attacked by Green and Shapiro for not being falsificationist enough, however, many rational choice theorists retreat behind Lakatosian claims (Green and Shapiro 1995a). Just as there are no atheists in foxholes, there are no naïve falsificationists in rejoinders. Lakatos's (1970) methodology of scientific research programmes holds that scientific theories comprise a hard core, a protective belt, and a positive and negative heuristic. The protective belt contains auxiliary hypotheses and initial conditions that protect the main assumptions of the programme from empirical refutation. The hard core is thus unfalsifiable. The positive and negative heuristics are rough guidelines as to which questions should and should not be pursued within the programme (Hands 2001, 112). Finally, assessment moves from the individual theory to a series of theories. One theory gives way to another when the new theory has excess content over the old theory. A research programme is scientific (progressive) if new theories with excess content replace old theories. A research programme is pseudoscientific (degenerative) if new theories with excess content do not replace old theories.

Although little mention of Lakatos is made by political scientists when not under attack, rational choice theorists who cite Lakatos are no less falsificationist than Green and Shapiro. Lakatos's goal was to defend Popper against the critiques of Kuhn (1970) and protect falsificationists from the embarrassing historical fact that theories are rarely jettisoned after being falsified (Hausman 1992, 85). Furthermore, Lakatos's views were meant to be descriptive, not prescriptive. The methodology of scientific research programmes more accurately describes the history of science than does the standard falsificationist account. Lakatos's achievement was to reconcile Popper with that history of science, and many of the problems faced by Popper are also faced by Lakatos (Hausman 1992, 192). If further evidence of the descriptive nature of Lakatos's contribution is needed, note that the relative merits of two research programmes can only be compared with hindsight (Chalmers 1982, 87). As a research programme is being developed, it is impossible to know whether it is progressive or degenerative.

It appears that in the conflict between Green and Shapiro and their critics, the critics won a battle or two, but Green and Shapiro won the war in the sense that many advocates of rational choice now argue for many of the same improvements in testing. The evidence that much of what Green and Shapiro argued for has come to pass lies both in Morton's (1999) *Methods and Models* and in the EITM initiative.

2.5.3 *Methods and Models*

Morton's (1999) methodological commitments are harder to pin down than Green and Shapiro's are. She finds value in both applied and pure theoretical models (22), empirical work informed by theory and not (22), and verified assumptions and false assumptions (142–45), but she provides no overarching justification for these perspectives. The constant throughout her book, however, is the importance of testing the deductive predictions of a model. A model, Morton writes, "is not evaluated if its predictions are not analyzed, regardless of how true the assumptions of the model are believed to be" (1999, 102).

With predictions as the key component in the evaluation of models, Morton lays out a set of steps to guide empirical analysis. Step 1 is "Understanding Assumptions." Note that step 1 is not "Test Assumptions" or "Verify Assumptions." In fact, Morton avers that false or nonverifiable assumptions are a hallmark of all models, and thus no political scientist should ever discard a model due to false assumptions (280). Step 2 is "Determining Predictions." Predictions are deductions from models, and models without predictions cannot be evaluated (280–81). Step 3 is "Examining Alternative Formal or Nonformal Models." Step 4 is "Choosing an Empirical Model." In this step, one must be careful to choose an empirical model whose assumptions do not change the predictions of the formal model (283). Step 5 is "Evaluating the Analysis." Models that pass the empirical test are supported, although full acceptance depends on the community of political scientists. Models that do not pass the empirical test are discarded or go through a process of post hoc adjustment (286).

What Morton describes in her five steps is a slightly more nuanced version of H-D. As assumption evaluation cannot be determinative (all models feature false or nonverifiable assumptions) and as multiple models are tested individually (284), the method boils down to deductive predictions and tests. Unlike Green and Shapiro, however, Morton does not advocate a strict version of falsificationism and notes that single disconfirming tests are rarely decisive.

2.5.4 The Empirical Implications of Theoretical Models

The EITM research initiative is a National Science Foundation (NSF) funded project to develop formal models that are tested with data. The program currently funds two summer institutes—attendance is *de rigueur* for advanced graduate students with technical training— as well as numerous individual projects. Thus, the NSF has invested substantial resources in the EITM initiative, and the next generation of political scientists will be greatly influenced by it. The goal of the initiative is to "bridge the gap" between formal and empirical analysis (National Science Foundation 2002, 5). As we trace the evolution of the initiative, we demonstrate that the "gap" is to be bridged using H-D.

The inception of EITM stems from a workshop convened by the Political Science Program of the NSF. The participants were "senior scholars with research experience in various technical-analytical areas and proven track records in activities that have improved the technical-analytical expertise in various sciences" (National Science Foundation 2002, 1). The essays written by the participants are hugely ironic as they make clear that the split between theory and empirical analysis is far from problematic. John Freeman argues that "the divide may be natural," and there exists "a natural division of labor in mature (viz., increasingly specialized) disciplines. So, to the extent such a divide exists, perhaps it is a sign of the maturation of our profession" (32). Henry Brady, while claiming that there exist good reasons for overcoming the split between formal theory and empirical modeling, argues that the split is fundamental and exists in physics and population ecology, and "in many other areas of science" (28). William Keech states that the split between formal theory and empirical modeling is not new and "to some extent it can be part of a healthy division of labor" and "not inappropriate" (36).

In the executive summary, however, this ambivalence gives way to statements such as "Significant scientific progress can be made by a synthesis of formal and empirical modeling" (13). In the mission statement of the 2008 EITM Summer Institute at Duke University, the claim is that "the scientific study of politics *requires* empirical evaluation of theoretical models" and that the gaps between theory and empirical analysis "seriously impair scientific progress" (*Overview* 2008; emphasis added). In a special issue of *Political Analysis*, Aldrich and Alt (2003, 310) claim that "the scientific study of politics requires the empirical testing of theoretical models, no less than any other scientific discipline." No citation or justification is given for this broad claim. Indeed, nowhere in this literature is a truly serious justification given for the necessity of combining theory and empirical analysis beyond claims that formal theories may be unrealistic and regressions atheoretic. At the same time, there are no serious justifications, beyond a few isolated examples, for how the lack of integration impedes science.

The clearest connection between H-D and the EITM movement is found in an article written by two scholars, Jim Granato and Frank Scioli, who are credited with bringing EITM to fruition (Aldrich and Alt 2003). Granato and Scioli (2004) are quite specific on the role that H-D should play in political science, and they elaborate their ideal world:

> In an ideal world, where there is unification in approach, political science research should have the following components: (1) theory (informed by case study, field work, or a "puzzle"); (2) a model identifying causal linkages; (3) deductions and hypotheses; (4) measurement and research design; and (5) data collection and analysis.
>
> (Granato and Scioli 2004, 315)

The H-D part of this ideal world is, of course, steps 3 and 5. In step 3, predictions are deduced from theories and written as hypotheses. In step 5, these predictions are tested to see if they hold. If the predictions hold, the model or theory gains credibility. If the predictions fail to hold, Granato and Scioli (2004, 314) are as ruthless as Green and Shapiro: "Theories must meet the challenges of these tests, and empirical work must be linked to a theory. Theories and concepts that fail are discarded."

For all the discussion of science in Granato and Scioli's article, there is no actual argument or justification for pursuing an EITM strategy. We are told, for instance, that "by thinking about the empirical implications of theoretical models, scholars develop clear-cut empirical tests" (Granato and Scioli 2004, 314). Although that statement may or may not be true, it is not an argument that scientific progress results from developing clear-cut empirical tests. That conclusion is simply assumed. The dangers of not pursuing an EITM strategy are illustrated with an anecdote regarding a mistake Milton Friedman made while working for Columbia University's Statistical Research Group during World War II. The authors hypothesize that Friedman might not have made his mistake if he had "used a statistical technique accompanied by a fully explicated formal model" (Granato and Scioli 2004, 318). This claim is pure conjecture. Friedman, himself, draws the lesson that "any hypothesis must be tested with data or nonquantitative evidence other than that used in deriving the regression or available when the

regression was derived" (Friedman and Schwartz 1991, 49). He makes
no mention of a formal model.

The frequently heard responses from proponents of the EITM
initiative when faced with criticism are that one, no one really knows
what EITM is; two, multiple understandings exist; and three, any
criticism is only meaningful to some other part of the project. These
responses, however, are insufficient when precious NSF dollars are at
stake and a generation of graduate students are being trained to follow
a particular method with weak justification.

2.6 CONCLUSION

Our goal in this chapter is to understand what is "scientific" about
current practice in political science. Our answer is that the claim
to "science" flows from the use of a particular method of inquiry:
hypothetico-deductivism. We demonstrate that a number of top
political scientists see their work through this lens and often encourage
others to do the same. We explain the method, show how thoroughly
it underlies much of our practice, and detail the pitfalls of following an
H-D strategy. We argue that there is little to be learned about a model
with false assumptions and that theoretical models are not tested with
data but with models of data. Finally, we explain how H-D became so
thoroughly enmeshed within our discipline. We trace its roots through
Riker and his understanding of logical positivism through more recent
examples including *Pathologies of Rational Choice Theory*, *Methods and
Models*, and the EITM project.

In the next chapter, we focus specifically on the concept of models
and how they should be understood. We argue that when understood
correctly, models perform a number of different functions, and in many
cases, testing models makes little sense. We argue for a different type of
model assessment and evaluation that moves the discipline away from
our current true-and-false dichotomy and toward an assessment based
on usefulness.

What Is a Model?

"What do you consider the *largest* map that would be really useful?"

"About six inches to the mile."

"Only *six inches!*" exclaimed Mein Herr. "We very soon got to six *yards* to the mile. Then we tried a *hundred* yards to the mile. And then came the grandest idea of all! We actually made a map of the country, on the scale of *a mile to the mile!*"

"Have you used it much?" I enquired.

"It has never been spread out, yet," said Mein Herr: "the farmers objected: they said it would cover the whole country, and shut out the sunlight! So we now use the country itself, as its own map, and I assure you it does nearly as well."

—Author LEWIS CARROLL

3.1 INTRODUCTION

Our claim in this book is that models are—and should be—the central feature of scientific reasoning in political science. Despite the ubiquity of models in political science, we understand little about their nature or how they operate. What a political scientist means when she uses the word *model* is rarely clear. She might, for example, be referring to the game that informs the theoretical side of her work. Or she might be referring to the regression equation in the empirical portion of her work. She might even be referring to the computational simulation she ran to investigate the assumptions she made in her game. She need not even be a quantitative researcher. After all, there exist constructivist models of international relations (Wendt 1992) and qualitative models of judicial decision making (Pogrebin 2003).

Despite all these uses of the term, most political scientists would be hard-pressed to provide a definition of model that encompasses these myriad uses. Discussions of models in political science primarily focus on their construction and composition, as opposed to what models are. We are told, in works too numerous to list, that models "abstract from reality," "simplify reality," and should "generate interesting hypotheses." We are told that models contain assumptions and predictions. Without an understanding of what a model is, however, we cannot understand why or how models perform these functions, or why they are constructed in a particular way.

In this chapter, we answer the question, "what is a model?" Our answer is that models should be viewed as tools or instruments, in particular, like maps.[1] Both models and maps display limited accuracy, partially represent reality, and most importantly, reflect the interest of the user. That is, models and maps are "purpose relative" (Morton 1993).

This analogy between models and maps should be familiar to social scientists. The authors of one well-known economics textbook explicitly use maps in a discussion of abstraction (Baumol and Blinder 2009). Even more to the point, the authors of a recent book on computational modeling write, "One of the best models that we encounter in our daily experience is the road map" (Miller and Page 2007, 36). Our approach should be considered an offshoot of the Semantic Conception of models, which was briefly introduced to the field by Henry Brady (2004b) in an introduction to a symposium on the science of politics. We begin with an extended discussion of maps, which draws on the work of Ronald Giere (1990, 1999).

3.2 MODELS AS MAPS

Consider the map of the Boston subway system in figure 3.1. If a tourist were to ask, "Is this map true?" a Bostonian might reasonably

Figure 3.1 Boston Subway Map, Prior to the Addition of the Silver Line. *The map is schematically similar to the Boston subway system. Subway riders find it useful, while pedestrians and drivers find it of little use. Map © 2005 Robert Schwandl (urbanrail.net) and reproduced with permission.*

respond, "True in what sense?" The tourist might then ask, "Well, is it accurate?" Again, the Bostonian might reasonably respond, "Accurate in what sense?" The exasperated tourist might finally ask "Is the map spatially correct?" and the answer to this question is "no." Any map that precisely reflected the facts on the ground would be as large as the area of interest and therefore useless. Any smaller map translates a three-dimensional object into a two-dimensional object. All maps are, therefore, inaccurate to some degree. Most people who inquire into the accuracy of a map, however, are not asking whether the map is spatially correct. Rather, what they really want to know is whether the map is similar enough to the facts on the ground to be used for the purpose of navigation. We still cannot answer this question in a general way, though. Whether the subway map is useful for navigation depends on the mode of transportation. The subway map is similar enough to the world to be used for the purpose of navigating the subway, but it is not similar enough to be used for other purposes, such as driving. As we will argue, the subway map is not rendered useless just because someone using it might make inaccurate predictions regarding the spatial layout of the Boston area.

As anyone who knows the Boston area will tell you, the subway map accurately reflects neither the spatial layout of the greater Boston area nor the spatial layout of the Boston subway system. Consider, for instance, the eastern side of the Red Line, which runs from South Station near the heart of the city to Braintree and Mattapan in the southeast. Looking at the map, you might assume that Mattapan is south of Braintree. In fact, Braintree is considerably farther south than Mattapan. By the same token, the eastern side of the Blue Line, which runs from Aquarium to Wonderland, is not actually straight but curves north at Suffolk Downs. Thus, the subway map does not accurately reflect either Boston or the subway system in any spatially accurate sense; some predictions based on it will be wrong.

The point here is not that visitors to Boston find themselves saddled with an inaccurate map of the area. The possibility of incorrect predictions does not make the map useless. Quite to the contrary, both commuters and tourists find the subway map uncommonly helpful. The problem lies not with the map but with the question. Asking whether the map is accurate (or true) is the wrong question. Instead, we should be asking whether the map is *useful*. Although not spatially accurate, the Boston subway map is very useful for navigating Boston's century-old subway system.

We do not argue, of course, that a map—or a model—can be completely divorced from reality and still be judged useful. The question then arises how similar does the map—or model—have to be to the real world to be useful. The answer is that it has to be similar enough to be useful for a particular purpose. The subway map has to be similar enough to the real-world subway system to make it useful for commuters and tourists. At this point, the reader may object to the similarity criterion. Two objects, after all, can be similar to one another in any number of ways. Doughnuts and coffee mugs are similar in the sense that they both have one hole. The similarity claim, however, need not be vague if the respects in which the two objects are similar and the degree to which they are similar are specified (Giere 1999, 4).

In what sense, then, is the Boston subway map similar to the Boston subway system? It is schematically similar. We can see the arrangement of stations on the Blue Line (Bowdoin to Wonderland), and we can see where the Blue Line intersects with the Orange Line (State) and the Green Line (Government Center). This kind of similarity makes the Boston subway map, despite its inaccuracies, useful for tourists who wish to navigate the city by subway. That is its purpose.

For other purposes, the Boston subway map is not similar enough to a particular real-world system to be useful. For instance, although a number of the stations are named for towns or cities, the spatial relationships between these stations and the towns or cities they represent are quite dissimilar. If one were interested in driving from town to town, for example, the subway map would prove completely useless. The spatial relationships between the towns on the map are not similar enough to the real world to be used for driving.

The road map in figure 3.2, however, is similar enough to the metro Boston road system to be used for driving. If you wanted to drive from the north shore of Boston, say, Revere, to the south shore, say, Quincy, this is the map you would want. Again, this map is inaccurate in an almost infinite number of ways, as a comparison between this map and a U.S. Geological Survey topographical map of the region would reveal. Many of the predictions based on this map would be wrong. The map is nonetheless useful for driving between towns. (It might be even more useful if it included exit markers.) On the other hand, the map is almost completely useless for navigating around Boston itself.

The most detailed map of Boston included here is the walking map in figure 3.3. Although this map is also inaccurate in its way (hundreds of small streets are missing, for example), it is useful if one intends

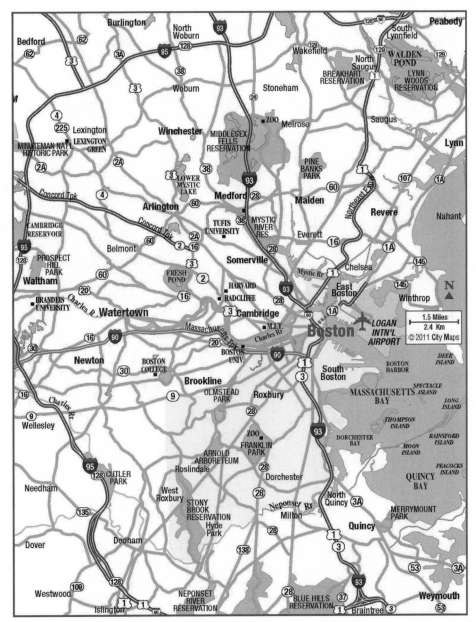

Figure 3.2 Boston Highway Map. *This map is useful for driving from town to town outside of Boston, but is of little use for driving in Boston or walking in Boston. Map © 2011 City Maps Inc. and reproduced with permission.*

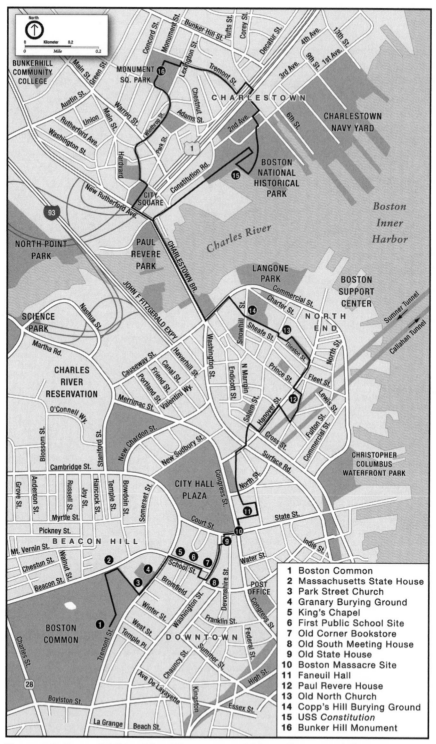

Figure 3.3 Boston Walking Map. *This map is useful for walking around downtown Boston, but is less useful for driving around downtown as none of Boston's many one-way streets are labeled. Map by Chris Erichsen.*

to walk the Freedom Trail (the numbered path in bold) from Boston Common to the Bunker Hill Monument. The map is of little use for driving around Boston, as many of the streets depicted in it are one-way. It is also of little use in navigating the subway system (none of the subway stops are marked). The usefulness of the map derives from its similarity to the street system of downtown Boston and the purpose for which it is designed: walking.

All three of these maps—the subway map, the driving map, and the walking map—have at least one area in common (downtown Boston). Each has a particular purpose, and each is useful for that purpose and pretty much that purpose alone. The subway map would quickly get you lost if you were driving and vice versa. The design element that makes these maps useful for a particular purpose is their partial nature. The maps contain little extraneous material that would add to the clutter but not to the usefulness. The walking map does not include subway stops, and the driving map does not include the sites of historical interest in downtown Boston. Although we could imagine (and have probably seen) dual-use maps, it is not necessarily true that such maps are more useful. A map that serves two purposes while maintaining a high degree of simplicity would be welcome, but generally there exists a trade-off between the number of purposes to which a map can be put and its simplicity. Usefulness is often a function of simplicity.

Our discussion of maps has raised a number of points that we should keep in mind when we talk about models.

- *Maps are objects and thus neither true nor false.* A map is an object. More specifically, it is an object that represents another object, a system in the real world. Like other kinds of objects (airplanes, coffee mugs, gas grills), maps are neither true nor false. They exist, and the question to ask of them, which is the same question we might ask of a coffee mug, is whether they are useful. Certain maps are useful in certain contexts and not in others.
- *Maps have limited accuracy.* As noted, each of our three maps has a large number of inaccuracies. In fact, when compared to

the real world, each map sports an infinite number of inaccuracies. The spatial relationships between features on the maps, for example, do not accurately reflect the spatial relationships that exist on the ground regardless of the purpose of the maps. In no case, however, do the inaccuracies impact the usefulness of the maps for the purpose for which they were designed. Accuracy and usefulness are simply two different concepts.

- *Maps are partial.* Maps represent some features of the world and not others. Which features are represented depends on the use to which the map is to be put. Walking maps do not include highway on-ramps and off-ramps, and highway maps do not include side streets. As previously argued, usefulness is a function of simplicity. When simplifying, however, attention must be paid to the purpose of the map. Some features are crucial. Eliminating side streets from a highway map makes understanding the map easier without damaging its usefulness. Leaving exit markers off of the map does not have the same result. Less simple or not, a highway map with exit markers is more useful than one without exit markers.

The major point made by our three examples is that

- *Maps are purpose-relative.* A map is designed to be similar enough to a system in the real world to be used for a specific purpose. That is, a map reflects the interests of those who designed it and those who use it. Whether a map is useful is a meaningless question unless one understands the purpose for which the map is to be used.

3.3 A FEW EXAMPLES FROM POLITICAL SCIENCE

The argument we are making is that we should view models in the same way that we view maps. That is, models should be viewed as objects and thus as neither true nor false. Models have limited accuracy and represent only certain features of a real-world system.

Most importantly, we argue that models are purpose-relative and that model assessment cannot take place without understanding the purpose for which the model was designed and used. The fact that a model makes incorrect predictions does not mean that it is useless. Asking whether a model is true or false is the wrong question; we need to ask whether a model is useful for the purpose for which it was intended.

To help fix these ideas, let's consider three important models of legislative policymaking: Keith Krehbiel's (1998) pivotal politics model, David Baron and John Ferejohn's (1989) divide-the-dollar model, and James Snyder and Tim Groseclose's (1996) vote-buying model. Like the three Boston maps, each of these models covers essentially the same territory: legislative policymaking. Also in keeping with the Boston maps, we argue that asking whether these models are true or false is the wrong question. We need to ask whether these models are useful for their particular purpose. Like the maps, these models have limited accuracy; none is a faithful representation of the legislative policymaking process, and yet these inaccuracies do not render the models less useful. These models are also partial as they exclude (or trivially include) key features of the legislative process, such as committees, bicameralism, and political parties. Nevertheless, these models are seen as important contributions to the legislative politics literature.

In Krehbiel's (1998) pivotal politics model, bargaining takes place over a proposal made by the median voter of the Senate. The proposal concerns a single policy (bargaining is therefore one-dimensional) and can be blocked by a filibuster, presidential veto, or both. Krehbiel (1998, 19) argues that his model fills a "basic need" by offering more reasonable results about the conditions under which policy gridlock is observed than the extant literature, which predicts either all gridlock or no gridlock. The model, however, is of very little use in understanding questions of distributive politics (the allocation of benefits to specific groups) or the role of interest groups in influencing policy outcomes.

Baron and Ferejohn's (1989) divide-the-dollar model features bargaining in which a proposer, chosen randomly from among all

legislators, makes a proposal to divide a fixed amount of public expenditures. In its simplest form, if the offer is rejected, a new proposer is
chosen, and this process continues until an agreement is reached. The
model offers insights into the role of the agenda setter and amendment
rules. Just as the Krehbiel model is of little help in understanding
distributive politics, the Baron and Ferejohn model focuses on a very
specific type of policy battle and has little to say about gridlock.

Groseclose and Snyder's (1996) vote-buying model is one where a
"vote buyer" (e.g., a party leader, interest group, the president) uses
resources to target members of a legislature. The vote buyer's goal
is to build a winning coalition in support of a piece of legislation.
Once this vote buyer has made offers to legislators, a second buyer,
who is on the opposite side of the issue, can make counteroffers.
The model demonstrates that coalitions larger than the minimum
needed to pass the bill are the norm in this setting. Unlike Baron
and Ferejohn, Groseclose and Snyder take the proposal as given and
therefore do not address the role of the agenda setter. Unlike Krehbiel,
Groseclose and Snyder do not address the role of the filibuster and the
presidential veto.

The analogy we draw between maps and models is quite sound.
Like maps, models are neither true nor false, they have limited
accuracy, they are partial, and most importantly, they are purpose-
relative. A researcher interested in understanding the role played by
the filibuster in policy debates will find both the Baron and Ferejohn
and Groseclose and Snyder models to be of little use. Those interested
in understanding distributive politics, on the other hand, will have little
use for either Krehbiel's model or Groseclose and Snyder's vote-buying
model. The important question to ask of a model is whether it is useful
for a particular purpose.

3.4 THE RECEIVED VIEW OF SCIENTIFIC THEORIES

What we are arguing may seem uncontroversial; after all, most any
scholar will tell you that his or her model is false in some respect. In our
view, however, stating that a model is false is a mischaracterization akin

to stating that a model is true. A model is an object, nothing more and nothing less. Philosophers of science have developed an approach to thinking about models that makes this point. The approach is known as the predicate or semantic conception of theories, and it is most closely associated with the work of Patrick Suppes (1967), Frederick Suppe (1977; 1989), Bas van Fraassen (1980), and Ronald Giere (1990).[2]

The important advance made by the semantic philosophers was to see models as objects and not as linguistic entities. To understand what a radical departure this was, we need some understanding of how an earlier, very influential group of philosophers of science viewed the role of theories in scientific reasoning. Briefly introduced in the previous chapter, these philosophers, known as logical positivists, saw theories as the central feature of scientific reasoning.[3] Theories, in their view, comprise a logical calculus and a set of "correspondence rules." Suppes (1967, 56) provides a succinct sketch of the account:

> A scientific theory consists of two parts. One part is an abstract logical calculus. In addition to the vocabulary of logic, this calculus includes the primitive symbols of the theory, and the logical structure of the theory is fixed by stating the axioms or postulates of the theory in terms of its primitive symbols. For many theories the primitive symbols will be thought of as theoretical terms like "electron" or "particle" that are not possible to relate in any simple way to observable phenomena.
>
> The second part of the theory is a set of rules that assign an empirical content to the logical calculus by providing what are usually called "co-ordinating definitions" or "empirical interpretations" for at least some of the primitive and defined symbols of the calculus.

Put another way, a scientific theory is "a set of uninterpreted sentences fabricated out of 'meaningless' symbols" (Schaffner 1969, 280). The correspondence rules provide an interpretation for the "meaningless" symbols. That is, they connect the nonlogical terms of the theory with empirical entities (Sloep and van der Steen 1987).[4]

More formally, the Received View holds that scientific theories comprise the following elements (Suppe 1989, 39–40). The main components are a first-order language L and a calculus K. The nonlogical constants of L are V_0, which contains the observation terms, and V_T, which contains the theoretical terms. L and K are divided into two subgroups corresponding to the observation language (L_0, which contains only V_0, and K_0) and the theoretical language (L_T, which contains only V_T, and K_T). A partial interpretation of the theoretical terms and of the sentences of L containing them is given by the theoretical postulates T, the axioms of the theory, and the correspondence rules C. The latter must be logically compatible with T and contain no extralogical terms not in V_0 or V_T. A scientific theory is denoted by TC, where T is the conjunction of the theoretical postulates, and C is the conjunction of the correspondence rules.[5]

Scientific theories, then, according to the logical positivists, are "partially interpreted axiomatic systems TC where the axioms T were the theoretical laws expressed in a theoretical vocabulary V_T; C were correspondence rules that connected T with testable consequences formulated using a separate observational vocabulary V_0" (Suppe 2000, S103). Under this view, a model is an interpretation of the theory such that the axioms of the theory are satisfied.

To make these ideas more concrete, consider Riker and Ordeshook's (1968) seminal paper "A Theory of the Calculus of Voting." Riker and Ordeshook are quite explicit about the deductive nature of their theory, as shown by the title of their article. Let R be the reward that an individual voter receives from her act of voting; B be the differential benefit that an individual voter receives from the success of her more preferred candidate over her less preferred one; C be the cost to the individual of the act of voting; P be the probability that the citizen will, by voting, bring about the benefit, B; and D be the satisfaction an individual feels when she has voted. Riker and Ordeshook state that these variables are related in the following lawlike fashion:

$$R = PB - C + D.$$

If $R > 0$, then it is rational to vote, and if $R \leq 0$, then it is not rational to vote. From this "law," the authors conclude that for those who do not vote, it must be that the cost of voting is greater than the instrumental value of voting, PB, plus the expressive value of voting D:

$$C > PB + D.$$

They also conclude that it always must be true that for those who vote, the instrumental value of voting must be greater than the difference between the cost of voting and the expressive value of voting:

$$PB > (C - D).$$

These mathematical expressions are part of the calculus of which logical positivists talk. The symbols R, B, C, P, and D are part of the nonlogical vocabulary. These terms must be interpreted for the calculus to have empirical content. When interpreted, these symbols stand for the various benefits and costs of voting.

Correspondence rules assign empirical content to the calculus by connecting it with the world of observation. Riker and Ordeshook (1968) operationalize P, the probability that the citizen will, in essence, affect the election outcome, with pre-election interview responses about how close the respondent believes the outcome of the presidential election would be.[6] B, the differential benefit from the success of the more preferred candidate, is measured by the pre-election responses as to how much the respondent "cares" about the outcome of the election. D, the satisfaction a voter feels from voting, is constructed out of four pre-election interview questions regarding the duty to vote. The cost of voting, C, is constructed out of D.[7]

The approach to thinking about theories just outlined is known as the Received View of scientific theories, and it is no surprise that the early formal modelers in political science found it attractive. The Received View, with its origins in classical mechanics, seemed a natural fit for scholars looking to put their young discipline on an equal footing with the "hard" sciences. When describing "formal, positive, political theory" in an application to the Center for Advanced Study in the Behavioral Sciences, Riker wrote, "By Formal, I mean the expression of the theory in algebraic rather than verbal symbols" (Bueno de Mesquita and Shepsle 2001, 8).

Soon after the publication of Riker and Ordeshook (1968), philosophers abandoned the Received View as a description of scientific theories.[8] The Received View was attacked on a host of grounds, two of which we mention here.[9] First, it was argued that not all theories can be meaningfully, or usefully, axiomatized. Suppe (1977, 64), for example, persuasively argues that "fruitful axiomatization of a theory is possible only if the theory to be axiomatized embodies a well-developed body of knowledge for which the systematic interconnections of its concepts are understood to a high degree." Many of the theories in the social sciences are just one set of examples given by Suppe where the state of theory development does not admit axiomatization. The precision involved in axiomatizing an informal theory would constitute an entirely new theory. Second, the idea of correspondence rules proved difficult (Sloep and van der Steen 1987, 3). Correspondence rules were thought to (a) define theoretical terms and (b) specify experimental procedures for applying theories to phenomena. In some cases, however, correspondence rules cannot capture the full meanings of theoretical terms, and more than one procedure for attributing meaning to theoretical terms could be found (Morrison and Morgan 1999a, 2). Additional problems included the reliance of correspondence rules on auxiliary theories (see our discussion of the Quine-Duhem problem in the previous chapter), and the implication that a change in the correspondence rules of a theory constitutes a new theory.

The Received View was also known as the Syntactic Conception because *syntax* refers to the relationship among symbols, and when the symbols are words, syntax refers to grammar. Thus, the Received View with its emphasis on the deductive structure of theories (the grammar, if you will) was, in essence, syntactic. The account that has developed in response to the Syntactic Conception is known as the Semantic Conception. Whereas *syntax* refers to the relationship among symbols, *semantics* refers to the relationship between symbols and the things for which the symbols stand (Salmon et al. 1992). The Semantic Conception, therefore, is concerned with the relationship between models and the actual world the models represent. The most important feature of the semantic account is that models, not theories, are central to the scientific enterprise.

3.5 THE SEMANTIC CONCEPTION OF SCIENTIFIC THEORIES

Although the Semantic Conception exists in a number of different versions, all agree on two points: one, models are neither true nor false; and two, models play the central role in science. Support for the Semantic Conception among philosophers of science is strong. Suppe (2000, S105) notes that "the Semantic Conception has been very successful. It is widely accepted with remarkably little published criticism of it—none fundamental or fatal." So widespread has been the support for the Semantic Conception that many consider it to be a "new received view" (Contessa 2011, 3).

The starting point of the Semantic Conception is Tarski's (1953, 11) definition of a model: "A possible realization in which all valid sentences of a theory T are satisfied is called a model of T." Thus, if a theory T contains axioms $A.1–A.3$, any structure in which those axioms are true is a model of T. Note that many different models can be consistent with T.[10] So a model under the semantic view could be a set-theoretical entity or a state space. This definition is a logician's sense of a model and comes from mathematical model theory, but Suppes (1961) argues that the concept of a model is the same in mathematics and the empirical sciences. His examples from the social sciences include quotes from Kenneth Arrow and Herbert Simon.

The semantic view comes basically in two flavors: one associated with Suppes (1961), and one associated with van Fraassen (1980). For Suppes, a model is a "set-theoretical entity which is a certain kind of ordered tuple consisting of a set of objects and relations and operations on these objects" (6). As an example, he presents a model of classical particle mechanics as an ordered tuple, $\mathcal{P} = <P, T, s, m, f>$, where P is a set of particles, T is an interval of real numbers corresponding to elapsed times, s is a position function defined on the Cartesian product of the set of particles in the time interval, m is a mass function, and f is a force function defined on the Cartesian product of the set of particles, the time interval, and the set of positive integers. The connection between this very abstract notion of a model and the phenomena being modeled is one of isomorphism. That is, the mathematical structure is isomorphic to a particular empirical system.

Van Fraassen (1980, 64) version of the semantic view also argues that to "present a theory is to specify a family of structures, its *models*; and secondly, to specify certain parts of those models (the *empirical substructures*) as candidates for the direct representation of observable phenomena." A model, according to van Fraassen, comprises three related elements: the possible states of the system using mathematical entities to represent these states in a state space, a set of elementary sentences that identify measurable physical magnitudes describing the physical system, and a satisfaction function that connects the state space with the elementary sentences (Minogue 1984, 115–16). Thus, "If X is a system of the kind defined by the theory, and there is a function '*loc*' that assigns a location in the state space T to X, then a model for the theory is the couple $< loc, X >$; that is, a model for the theory involves the assignment of the location in the state space of the theory to a system of the kind defined by the theory" (Thompson 1989, 80).[11] As in Suppes's version, the relation between the model and the physical system is one of isomorphism.

The previous two paragraphs are arguably the most confusing and technical in this book, and both accounts seem to have little to do with how scientists actually use models. As a corrective, we turn to what we call the model-based view, which, although based on the semantic view, is far less abstract and is similar to the ways some prominent economists view models (see Hausman 1992 and Mäki 2009). We focus on work by Ronald Giere, who presents an admirably clear version of the model-based view. Giere, like Suppes and van Fraassen, insists that models are neither true nor false and contends that theories are collections of models. He differs from Suppes and van Fraassen in replacing isomorphism with similarity relations and rejecting an axiomatic approach to theory (Morrison and Morgan 1999a).

3.6 THE MODEL-BASED VIEW OF SCIENTIFIC THEORIES

A *model*, according to Giere (1990), is a system characterized by a definition, and by a definition, he means a stipulation. That is, a model stipulates how certain terms are to be used. Just as a definition is constructed—Nelson Goodman constructed the definition of his term *grue* (see chapter 2)—a stipulation is an agreement on the meaning of important terms. A model, therefore, is constructed or defined by a researcher. When a model includes equations, one might be tempted to ask if the model is true, but that question is not the right one to ask. The model is defined as a system that exactly satisfies the equations (Giere 1990, 78–79). Giere's example is the simple harmonic oscillator, which is a system that satisfies the law

$$F = -kx.$$

The law states that a restoring force, F, is proportional (k is a positive constant) to the displacement, x.

The simple harmonic oscillator is neither true nor false; it is a system that satisfies the equation. For a more complex example, consider the following model: "A Newtonian Particle System is a system that satisfies the three laws of motion and the law of universal gravitation" (Giere 1984, 81). That is, the model *asserts* that a system is a Newtonian Particle System if the system satisfies the three laws of motion and the law of universal gravitation. The stipulation can be more complicated and more specific:

We can define a Newtonian theoretical model that may be used to represent the Earth/Moon system. This model would consist of two masses, one having about 1/80 the mass of the other and located approximately 240 thousand miles away. Depending on the exact masses, distances, and velocities that we specify, the laws defining the Newtonian Particle System would tell us the exact behavior of such a system. There is no need to cite evidence to justify claims about the behavior of the model and its component particles.

(Giere 1984, 81)

For an example oriented toward political science, we consider a model of distributive politics, a phrase that refers to the allocation of government projects or programs that benefit specific groups or legislative districts. Scholars doing research in distributive politics generally concern themselves with explaining either the outcomes of bargaining or the roles various institutions play in producing the outcomes of the bargaining process. Those in the first group ask which groups or legislative districts receive projects and why, ask whether the projects are efficient, and inquire into the level of total spending, given a minimal legislative structure. Those in the second group ask what is the role of bicameralism, what is the role of an executive with veto power, and what is the role of political parties. The Baron and Ferejohn (1989) paper discussed earlier is a classic of the distributive politics literature. Here, though, we discuss the work of Ansolabehere, Snyder, and Ting (2003), who build on the Baron and Ferejohn model by including a bicameral legislature. At the same time, these authors circumscribe the previous model by assuming that no amendments to a proposal are allowed (that is, a closed rule) and that legislators are perfectly patient (that is, no discounting occurs).

The model takes the form of a definition or stipulation. There is a lower chamber (a House) where members represent districts with equal population within a state. There is an upper chamber (a Senate) where members represent entire states. Each district has one representative, and each state has one senator. Public expenditures can be divided down to the district level, legislators are responsive to their median voters, and both chambers vote by majority rule. The actual bargaining takes the following form: a member of the House is selected at random to propose a division of the public expenditures. If a majority of each chamber votes in favor of the proposal, it passes, and the game ends. If the proposal fails, a new proposer is chosen at random to make a proposal. The game continues until a proposal is successful.

Note that this model is based on a stipulation, and there is no way to falsify it—it is a definition.[12] As in Giere's example, there is no need for evidence to justify the claims of the model. The outcome is determined by the original definition and whatever values we specify for the unknown parameters. The question we should ask of this model is not whether it is "true," but rather, is it similar in certain respects, and for certain uses, to a system in the real world.

The relationship between a model and a real-world system is asserted by the *theoretical hypothesis*. Where a model defines a certain class of systems, a theoretical hypothesis asserts that certain (sorts of) real systems are among members of that class (van Fraassen 1989). Such a hypothesis takes the following form: "A model M is similar to system S in certain respects and degrees" (Morrison and Morgan 1999a, 4). In other words, a theoretical hypothesis asserts that an object, a system known as a model, is similar, in some respect and for some purpose, to another object, a real-world system. Objections are often raised because similarity is a notoriously tricky concept. As noted earlier in the chapter, any object is similar to any other object in some respects and to some degree, and as previously argued, a similarity claim is not vacuous provided the respects and degree to which two objects are similar is specified explicitly. Giere (1990, 81) provides the following example: "The positions and velocities of the earth and moon in the earth-moon system are very close to those of a two-particle Newtonian model with an inverse square central force."

As Giere points out, "position" and "velocity" are the respects in which the Newtonian model and the earth-moon system are similar. The degree to which these two systems, one abstract and one real, are similar is "very close." Although the theoretical hypothesis is a linguistic entity, and thus true or false, its testability is not particularly important. The hypothesis claims only that "an indicated type and degree of similarity exists between a model and a real system. We can therefore forget about truth and focus on the details of the similarity" (Giere 1990, 81).

To return to the Ansolabehere, Snyder, and Ting example, a theoretical hypothesis asserts some degree of similarity between the model and the distribution of public expenditures by the U.S. Congress. The authors are quite explicit about the respects in which and the degree to which their model is similar to bargaining in Congress. Bicameralism is clearly an important point of similarity. The authors argue that the application of previous research featuring a single chamber is significantly limited. "Strictly speaking, none of these models apply, for example, to the U.S. Congress or to 49 of the American states" (Ansolabehere, Snyder, and Ting 2003, 472). They also point out that just as in the U.S. Congress, geographic areas of representation are nested in their model (473). In addition, they note that simple majority rule in their model "approximates the behavior of legislators in practice" (473).

At the same time, the authors are quite explicit about the ways their model is not similar to bargaining in the U.S. Congress. They point out that the closed rule is a special case, and they argue that they can safely ignore modeling the resolution of differences between the chambers because it "adds a layer of complication that is not needed to gain important insights" (473). They choose to model the upper chamber as having only one member from each state. Moreover, by considering only bills that are entirely distributive in nature, they capture only a small part of actual legislation. The point of the theoretical hypothesis is not to claim that models that fail to include bicameralism are "false," or that modeling open amendment rules is unimportant. Rather, the theoretical hypothesis states the extent to which the model is similar to a particular real-world system and for what purpose. Ansolabehere, Snyder, and Ting are interested in the effects of bicameralism on bargaining, and for that purpose, bicameralism is of course important, and open amendment rules are not. The theoretical hypothesis is neither vague nor vacuous.

The results they obtain by making these choices provide significant insight into the distribution of public expenditures under bicameralism. Conventional wisdom holds that small states are advantaged in distributive bargaining because they have equal representation in the Senate—a senator from Rhode Island has the same voting power as a senator from California—and therefore can obtain greater resources for their state than their size would suggest. Contrary to this wisdom, the authors show that in their primary model, small states have no advantage in bargaining, despite their disproportionate influence in the upper chamber.[13] In building the cheapest coalition possible in the House, the proposer simultaneously constructs a winning coalition in the Senate (because the benefits going to districts benefit the states in which those districts are located). So, no projects need to be awarded with the single goal of attracting the support of a senator.

3.7 MODELS AND THEORIES

Our discussion of the model-based view defined what a model is (a definition) and how models are connected to reality (theoretical hypotheses). Although we have noted that under this account theories are collections of models, we feel the need to expound upon this point given the ubiquity with which the term theory is used in political science. We do so with the understanding that more than one leading proponent of the semantic view has argued that the issue is unimportant (Suppes 1967, 63). We begin with another discussion of the harmonic oscillator model.

> At its most abstract the linear oscillator is a system with a linear restoring force, plus any number of other, secondary forces. The simple harmonic oscillator is a linear oscillator with a linear restoring force and no others. The damped oscillator has a linear restoring force plus a damping force. And so on. Similarly, the mass-spring oscillator identifies the restoring force with the stiffness of an idealized spring. In the pendulum oscillator, the restoring force is a function of gravity and the length of the string. And so on. . . .

"The linear oscillator," then, may best be thought of not as a single model with different specific versions, but as a *cluster* of models of varying degrees of specificity. Or, to invoke a more biological metaphor, the linear oscillator may be viewed as a family of models, or still better, a family of families of models.

(Giere 1990, 79–80)

That is, a *theory*, according to the semantic view, is a collection of models or "a set of models" (Salmon 1988, 6). More specifically, Giere (1990, 85) defines a theory as "comprising two elements: (1) a population of models, and (2) various hypotheses linking those models with systems in the real world." A theory, then, is not a well-defined entity, and there are no rules regarding which models are included in a particular theory. This use of the term *theory* seems very much in line with casual usage by political scientists. A recent review of democratic peace theory, for example, lists six different "logics" nested within the theory (Rosato 2003). These include one normative logic (norm externalization leads to mutual trust and respect) and five institutional logics (public constraint, group constraint, slow mobilization, surprise attack, and information, all of which work through an accountability process). Similarly, a recent view of realism attempts to come to terms with the myriad positions encompassed by the term (Bell 2008).

The relationship between a theory and the models that comprise the theory is depicted in figure 3.4. A real-world system, S, is characterized by m features, f_j, $j = 1, \ldots, m$. In terms of the Ansolabehere, Snyder, and Ting example, the system is the legislative bargaining process in Congress. The features of the system include bicameralism, nested representation, particular amendment rules, and many others. The theory, T, is characterized by n models, M_i, $i = 1, \ldots, n$, and k theoretical hypotheses, TH_l. Each theoretical hypothesis states the respects in which and the degree to which its respective model is similar to the system, S. The arrows indicate which features of the system are included in the different models (and we have to imagine that the arrows can tell us the degree of similarity). If M_1 were the Ansolabehere, Snyder, and Ting model, the arrows would be pointing

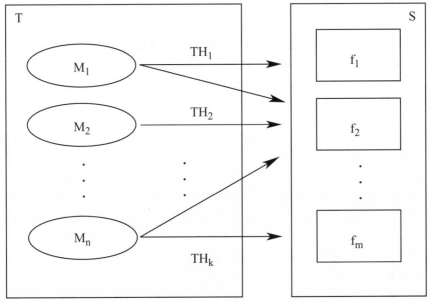

Figure 3.4 The Relationship between a Theory, Its Models, and a Real-World System. *A theory, T, comprises n models, M_i, and k theoretical hypotheses, TH_l. A real-world system, S, comprises m features, f_j, which can be modeled.*

at bicameralism and nested representation. To be clear, the arrows themselves are not the theoretical hypotheses, but we can think of the collection of arrows emanating from a single model as its theoretical hypothesis. Note that the theory, T, encompasses the models and the theoretical hypotheses, but not the real-world system.

To return to our example, the "theory of distributive politics" is really a family of models concerned with the distribution of public expenditures among competing actors. Like harmonic oscillator "theory," distributive politics "theory" includes both basic and very abstract models as well as more sophisticated models. The earliest models include Riker (1962) and Buchanan and Tullock's (1962) seminal work on coalition building. The models provide the basic logic for understanding why minimum-winning coalitions (the smallest group large enough to impose its will) form when dividing a fixed amount of public expenditures. Weingast (1979) explains why legislatures develop norms whereby individual legislators can pick projects for their districts with little interference from the rest of the legislature. The reasons include uncertainty regarding the composition of the minimum-winning coalition, and the fact that the amount of public expenditures to be divided is not fixed (leading to non–zero-sum bargaining).

Later models focused more on institutions. Baron and Ferejohn (1989) created a framework for focusing on the role of amendment rules on spending in a noncooperative bargaining environment. Numerous other models both expand and circumscribe that model. Diermeier and Feddersen (1998), for instance, look at the vote of confidence procedures in parliamentary systems, and McCarty (2000) looks at an executive with veto power. Chari, Jones, and Marimon (1997) include voters in an effort to study split-ticket voting. Battaglini and Coate (2007) address distortionary taxation and public goods spending, whereas Snyder, Ting, and Ansolabehere (2005) incorporate weighted voting.

Note the relationship between the collection of models just described and the three maps discussed earlier in the chapter. Like the three maps, the distributive politics models cover essentially the same ground but from different perspectives. That multiple models describe the same object is quite natural; there is no such thing as the one, true model. George Stibitz (1966, 41), one of the fathers of modern digital computing, writes,

> The fact I want to bring out is that, for the same physical object or phenomenon, there are many conceivable models. These models may range through many orders of complexity and through many degrees of completeness or of precision. There is no unique correspondence between a thing and its model. Just as a circular cylinder may serve as a model for a glass tube, for a copper tube or for a hole in a block of steel, so a model for the glass tubing may be a simple cylinder, an irregular geometric form or even a statistical distribution of mathematical points.

Thus, these models of distributive politics have limited accuracy and are purposefully partial; they are not sequential in the sense that later models do not always incorporate all the features present in earlier models. They are purpose-relative; the authors choose the level of abstraction and list of features to be modeled with a particular purpose in mind. Taken together, they comprise the theory of distributive politics.

What are the precise boundaries of distributive politics theory? Which models should be included in the theory, and which should be excluded? These are the wrong questions to ask. There are no definitive answers to these questions, and it is precisely in this sense that we are arguing that models should occupy pride of place in scientific reasoning. Precisely delineating the boundaries of distributive politics theory is unnecessary. What matters is evaluating the extent to which these models fulfill the purposes for which they were intended.

3.8 CONCLUSION

Dissenters may claim that our argument here amounts to nothing more than a change in language. What we used to call theories we should now call models. Even if that were the case, it would be a contribution. After all, "model" and "theory" are the terms we use to communicate with one another. However, our argument has important implications beyond the semantic ones. The most sweeping of these implications relates to the evaluation of models, and to determine whether a model fulfills the purpose for which it was intended, we need to understand the various roles models can play. To that end, we discuss theoretical models and statistical models separately, for although they are all models, they often serve quite different purposes. We detail those purposes in the next two chapters.

Theoretical Models

The sciences are the children of our minds; we must allow each one of them to develop naturally, and not force them into molds that are not appropriate for them.

—Nobel Prize-winning economist ROBERT AUMANN

4.1 INTRODUCTION

In the previous chapter, we argued that models should be assessed based on their usefulness for a specific purpose. In this chapter and the next, we detail the purposes to which models can be put, offering examples from political science and economics. To do this, we divide models into two groups, theoretical and statistical, focusing on theoretical models in this chapter.[1] We also offer some guidance for judging whether a model is useful.

What we do not offer in this chapter is an arbitrarily precise formulation for assessing usefulness or determining that one model is more useful than another. Cartwright (1983, 11) eloquently states the problem with such an approach:

In physics, it is usual to give alternative theoretical treatments of the same phenomenon. We construct different models for different purposes, with different equations to describe them. Which is the right model, which the "true" set of equations? The question is a mistake. One model brings out some aspects of the phenomenon; a different model brings out others.

Some equations give a rougher estimate for a quantity of interest, but are easier to solve. No single model serves all purposes best.

In other words, which model is "best" depends on the intended use. Different models highlight different aspects of the phenomenon under study, and there is no such thing as the "right" model. This statement is as true of theoretical models as it is of empirical models. Until we realize that it is impossible to understand any phenomenon fully through a single set of models (one theoretical and one empirical), the discipline cannot move forward.

Before delving into a discussion of how models vary by purpose, we highlight three other important characteristics of theoretical models: their reliance on deductive reasoning, their construction, and their level of abstraction.

4.2 ASPECTS OF THEORETICAL MODELS

Deductive reasoning. Theoretical models typically rely in one way or another on deductive reasoning.[2] By *deductive reasoning*, we refer to the derivation of statements that follow necessarily from an initial set of statements (Boyd, Gasper, and Trout 1993, 776). For instance, from the first three statements below, we can derive the fourth:

1. Democracies do not wage war against one another.
2. The United States and Iraq fought a war.
3. The United States is a democracy.
4. Iraq was not a democracy at the time the war was initiated.

For the argument to be valid deductively, statement 4 must be true if statements 1, 2, and 3 are true. (Recall that in chapter 2 we referred to the truth-preserving quality of a deductive system.) Doron and Sened (2001, 146) write, "Deductive reasoning has one clear advantage over inductive reasoning—it need not be verified in the empirical world. In fact, it need not even reflect real world phenomena. Its falsification comes about as a result of internal inconsistency." Put another way, "the assumptions and derived statements of a model, then, are not themselves propositions that can be true or false, roughly true or wildly off the mark" (Gibbard and Varian 1978, 667). Empirical accuracy is not in question when it comes to deductive arguments. Usefulness is.

Technique. Formal theoretical models in political science rely on the techniques of social choice theory and game theory, among others. These approaches differ in substantial ways. Social choice theory, for instance, focuses on "direct preference aggregation" in nonstrategic settings, and game theory focuses on "indirect preference aggregation through the aggregation of choices in strategic settings" (Austen-Smith and Banks 1998, 284). A social choice model, for example, might take a set of individual preferences and map them into a collective choice using a voting rule. A game theoretic model might embed the individuals with these preferences into a sequential voting model in which several proposals can be made until one is agreed on, allowing for a deep analysis of strategy. These approaches begin with a set of assumptions and combine these assumptions with a solution concept. A common solution concept in game theory, for example, is the Nash equilibrium.

Those who construct "informal" or verbal models engage in an enterprise similar to those who work with game theoretic models. Clear verbal models can be just as useful as the most complex mathematical models, depending on the purpose to which they are put. Although this chapter focuses on mathematical theoretical models, the argument extends equally well to verbal models.

Level of abstraction. How much a theoretical model abstracts from reality lies on a continuum. Some models bear close resemblance to a few key features of the real world even as they abstract away from others. These more applied models focus on particular features unique to an area of inquiry, such as models used to answer questions about a specific country, legislature, or bargaining setting. One cannot, for example, understand decision making in the U.S. Senate without capturing the many opportunities (most notably the filibuster) available to senators wishing to hold up legislation. Similarly, it might be argued that a model of U.S. policymaking intent on capturing legislative bicameralism ought to account for the overlap between districts in the lower chamber and those in the upper chamber. Of course, the advantage of applied models might also be viewed as a disadvantage. By focusing on particular institutional features, the applicability of the model to other institutions or situations may be unclear.

At the other end of the continuum are models that are worlds unto themselves, largely divorced from reality, that serve as thought experiments. The strength of these models lies in their lack of isomorphism with the real world. Economists often view models as artificial worlds through which ideas may be explored. Gibbard and Varian (1978, 665) describe such models as "ideal models" that are a "description of some ideal case which is interesting either in its own right or by comparison to reality." The model of perfect competition in economics is an example of an ideal model. It assumes that products are identical, entry and exit into the market is costless, and no positive or negative economies of scale exist (i.e., the size of the firm does not influence production costs). In political science, the spatial model of two-party competition, in which both parties and all voters have complete information about preferences and policy promises are always credible, is an ideal model. Returning to the filibuster example, an ideal model of legislatures might feature some generic set of veto rights, of which the filibuster might be a special case.

Critics of formal modeling in political science often view ideal models as intellectual games with nothing to offer beyond mathematical elegance. Similar critiques are leveled at models in economics. Economist theorist Robert Sugden agrees that theoretical models have the potential to be mathematical exercises with little scientific upside (Sugden 2001). To ignore all such models, though, is problematic. Sugden views models that may appear divorced from reality—"abstract and unrealistic and ... lead[ing] to no clearly testable hypotheses"— as nonetheless being valuable if they tell us something about the world (2). He provides two examples of such models in economics: Akerlof's market for lemons and Schelling's checkerboard model of racial segregation. These models are highly abstract and divorced from the real world, and yet the models can be used for "conceptual exploration" that ultimately informs our understanding of reality.

Akerlof's model shows that under asymmetric information about the quality of a used car, the market for cars should continually contract until it ultimately collapses. According to Sugden, the model is a representation of markets that underscores the problems with standard economic models that assume symmetric information about product quality. Schelling's checkerboard model of segregation shows that even if (1) most people do not wish to segregate, and (2) public policy is neutral with respect to segregation, then communities nevertheless can be partitioned as long as individuals want some minimal level of overlap with similar individuals (with "similar" defined along any dimension one likes—race, ideology, etc.). The model illustrates how individually reasonable behavior can lead to collectively suboptimal results (if diversity is a goal).

Ideal worlds also help establish benchmarks against which the real world can be judged. That is, through the examination of ideal worlds, we can begin to understand how reality falls short of some goal. Consider the problem of negative externalities occurring as the by-product of economic behavior. The quintessential example is pollution that is the by-product of production but is not factored into market prices for a good. Economic theory, undoubtedly an ideal world, has long held that we can design tax schemes that force producers and consumers to account for the effect of production on pollution levels. Alternatively, governments could set a level of pollution and then create a tradable permits market that encourages firms to reduce pollution levels. Both solutions, however, rely on an assumption that governments possess the requisite information (such as what "optimal" pollution levels are and precisely how individuals and producers will respond to a tax) to implement the reforms. In addition, policies are not made by a benevolent central planner, but by legislators and politicians who may not act in economically efficient ways. Despite these dissimilarities with the real world, ideal models of externalities are useful for establishing the conditions under which pollution can be reduced to efficient levels through government intervention and have shaped how we view and understand reform attempts in the real world.

4.3 THE PURPOSES OF MODELS

There are many ways to categorize models: by technique (social choice theory versus game theory), informational assumptions (complete information versus incomplete information), field of study (legislative models versus models of war), the nature of the interaction (cooperative versus noncooperative), and so on. Just as models should be assessed by whether they are useful for a specific purpose, so too ought a categorization of models be judged in this way.[3] In constructing a typology of models focusing on *purpose*, we provide a foundation for thinking about the *usefulness* of political science models. None of the foregoing categorizations speak both to usefulness and purpose in categorizing models. What we present here does.[4]

Models serve in any one (or more) of four different roles: foundational, organizational, exploratory, and predictive.[5] We do not place *normative models*, the purpose of which is to make claims about what ought to be, into a separate category because the normative analyses performed in political science or economics—for example, evaluating whether a voting rule satisfies certain normatively desirable properties—can only be understood in the context of theoretical models. In other words, to conduct a normative analysis requires a model that fits into one of the above categories. Consider, for example, a researcher who wishes to argue for a society that has end result x, where x might refer to equality of wealth or free markets. There are two components to the argument. The first is to establish why such a society is desirable normatively. The second is to demonstrate what sorts of societies are likely to produce such outcomes. For instance, many models with normative motivations fit into the exploratory camp. If a goal is to ensure equality of wealth, then it will be useful to construct exploratory economic models establishing what sorts of economic institutions are likely to produce such an outcome.

Second, normative considerations factor into the modeling enterprise by structuring the kinds of questions political scientists and
economists ask. Perhaps the best example is the concept of Pareto
optimality, an allocation of resources under which no person can be
made better off without making someone else worse off. Economists
tend to focus on Pareto-optimal allocations of resources when working
with economic models. Yet Pareto optimality ignores *distributional*
concerns about who gets what.

4.3.1 Foundational Models

Foundational models serve one of two related purposes: providing
a result that serves as the basis for further model building, or
constructing a framework that is flexible enough to be adapted to
answer many different kinds of questions. Such models may not reflect
any real-world situation, and yet may still provide the researcher with
important insights. Often, foundational models are created to answer
other questions and fit into other categories, but they are given new
meaning (and a new purpose) by virtue of their impact on subsequent
research.

As an example of a model that achieves both objectives, consider
Arrow's Theorem, one of the most important results in the study
of collective choice. Arrow (1963) demonstrates that there is no
collective choice rule that can translate all possible configurations
of individual preferences into a group choice coherently—short of
making one individual a dictator. He proves this result in a highly
stylized environment with no institutional structure or strategic
motivations on the part of voters. In short, the model is truly that
of an "idealized" world.

Arrow specifies his question clearly: "We ask if it is formally possible
to construct a procedure for passing from a set of known individual
tastes to a pattern of social decision-making, the procedure in question
being required to satisfy certain natural conditions" (Arrow 1963, 2).
This deceptively simple question created an entire field of research. His
result has been modified, attacked, revised, and reworked for decades,

all of which is a testament to its importance. Once Arrow established that no such procedure existed, he laid the foundation for a series of follow-up questions:

1. Does a consistent procedure exist if one of the conditions is relaxed?
2. What happens if voters are strategic?
3. Can placing an institutional structure on decision making eliminate the problem of incoherence in group decision making?
4. What are the implications of this result for the design of election rules?[6]

These questions range from the applied (the design of real-world election systems) to the abstract (incorporating strategic voters into Arrow's framework). Directly building on this model, Gibbard (1973) and Satterthwaite (1975) establish that any procedure violating one of Arrow's conditions is subject to manipulation by strategic voters. Not only are collective choice procedures prone to violating basic ideas of "fairness," but these violations can be leveraged by voters to help their preferred alternative emerge victorious.

Foundational models also provide a framework that is flexible enough to be of use to scholars in answering substantive questions. Baron and Ferejohn's (1989) model of legislative bargaining has been used as the foundation for dozens of applications and extensions. Their game theoretic model examines how a dollar is distributed among a group of legislators interested in maximizing their share of the pie. Their legislature is highly stylized: there are no parties, disputes over social policy, or even debates about the size of overall spending. Nonetheless the model is able to demonstrate the power of the agenda setter in bargaining settings, the role of patience in bargaining when delay is possible, and the impact of amendments on agenda setter power. Baron and Ferejohn's simple framework has allowed researchers to probe questions related to weighted voting (e.g., Snyder, Ting, and Ansolabehere 2005), government formation in parliamentary democracies (e.g., Baron 1991), and the provision of pork-barrel projects versus public goods in legislatures (e.g., Battaglini and Coate 2007), to name a few. The model's virtue is the minimal structure that Baron and Ferejohn impose on bargaining. This "ideal model" proved flexible and therefore useful in a variety of theoretical and applied settings.

In the international relations literature, Putnam's (1988) two-level game serves the role of a foundational model. Putnam refers to his game as a "metaphor" and calls on future scholars to create game theoretic models capturing the two-level dynamic inherent in international negotiations. He writes,

> The politics of many international negotiations can usefully be conceived as a two-level game. At the national level, domestic groups pursue their interests by pressuring the government to adopt favorable policies, and politicians seek power by constructing coalitions among those groups. At the international level, national governments seek to maximize their own ability to satisfy domestic pressures, while minimizing the adverse consequences of foreign developments. Neither of the two games can be ignored by central decision-makers, so long as their countries remain interdependent, yet sovereign. . . . The unusual complexity of this two-level game is that moves that are rational for a player at one board (such as raising energy prices, conceding territory, or limiting auto imports) may be impolitic for that same player at the other board.
>
> (Putnam 1988, 434)

Putnam foreshadows the difficulty of constructing solutions to these games, but numerous scholars have forged ahead. Grossman and Helpman (1995) model how leaders negotiate trade agreements and set trade policy given the competing domestic goals of helping the general electorate and securing campaign contributions from interests who may prefer protectionism. Mo (1994) studies the conditions under which a negotiator in international bargaining, such as the president, would want to grant veto authority to an agent, such as Congress, and Mo (1995) models international bargaining when domestic coalitions to support such agreements are formed endogenously. Pahre (1997) builds on the intuition that domestic politics can constrain negotiators in the international arena by constructing a model of parliamentary democracy in which government formation is endogenous and constrains the negotiator. Milner (1997) proposes a two-level model that emphasizes how domestic institutions shape which interests are favored and policies chosen, in turn influencing international agreements. She argues that existing models have had a limited impact on the international relations literature due to a dearth of testable hypotheses, thus demonstrating yet again the unfortunate consequences of focusing on testability when evaluating the usefulness of models.

Two-level games have fallen out of favor in international relations in recent years, in part because they are complicated to solve beyond a basic setup. Still, this simple logic—that international bargaining affects domestic activities, and that domestic activities are shaped by expectations about their influence on international bargaining—has generated important insights about domestic and international politics.

4.3.2 Organizational Models

Models that play an organizational role provide a "framework wherein information may be defined, collected and ordered" (Haggett and Chorley 1967). One purpose of such a model might be to collect a group of disparate empirical generalizations or known facts under a single framework. The simple prospective model of voting and party identification in Achen (1992) plays precisely this role. Achen's model makes three assumptions: voters are rational, voters are prospective in orientation, and there exist two parties that offer benefits to voters that vary over time around a constant though unknown mean (thus, voters have to estimate the mean based on previous experience). The estimation process forms the basis for an individual's party identification. Achen derives eleven propositions from his model, ten of which had already been established by previous scholarship. Thus, his model "subsumes within a unified framework a broad range of findings in the literature" (Achen 1992, 206). These findings include that the party identification of new voters tends to be correlated with that of their parents but is more centrist and more subject to change, and party identification changes only when shocks to the previous period's level of benefits occur. Achen refers to the deductive link between his model and the eleven empirical generalizations as "validating the model" (204); this phrase is ambiguous, but in no way does the organizational role of the model serve to establish its "accuracy."

Organizational models are also found in the international relations literature. Bueno de Mesquita and Lalman (1992) present five empirical puzzles, including the fact that democracies rarely fight with one another. They write, "The sundry observations about democratic politics and international conflict are rich with empirical puzzles but are not yet similarly enriched by an encompassing theory that helps make sense of the seemingly disparate, anomalous, and even contradictory observations that have been made" (145–46). They view their model as making "sense of the diverse empirical findings reported thus far" (146).

This same perspective is evident in Bueno de Mesquita et al. (2003). The authors propose a "selectorate" model in which leaders hold political power by maintaining a winning coalition within the group of individuals—the selectorate—who choose the leaders. They explore how changes in the sizes of winning coalitions and selectorates, as well as the ratio between these two figures, alter both domestic and international politics. They view the model as "facilitat[ing] the derivation of both well-established empirical regularities and new propositions regarding governance and political economy" (11–12). These empirical regularities include the "known empirical regularities collectively called the *democratic peace*," for which they claim their model provides a "comprehensive account" (13). Specifically, the authors believe that their selectorate model offers a "logically coherent account" for at least seven tendencies related to the democratic peace, including the findings that democracies tend to win wars, regularly fight with nondemocracies, and engage in shorter wars than nondemocracies when they do fight.[7]

A model that provides a general framework for deriving a range of existing theoretical models is also organizational.[8] This sort of model illustrates the connections between models, thereby aiding the accumulation of knowledge.[9] To give an example, Banks and Duggan (2000) solve a multidimensional spatial model using the bargaining procedure established in Baron and Ferejohn (1989). They show that different versions of the divide-the-dollar game, the spatial model, and models of public goods and exchange economies can all be understood within this framework. Additionally, their model produces versions of Black's (1958) Median Voter Theorem and Downs's (1957) party competition results.

A model that generalizes an existing set of models may demonstrate precisely how the assumptions of those models drive their results. For instance, Bendor and Meirowitz (2004) argue that existing models of delegation rest on several convenient assumptions. By developing an overarching framework for understanding delegation, Bendor and Meirowitz are able to establish how sensitive a model's results are to various assumptions.

Organizational models are also used to describe the world by creating a classification system or a way to rank cases on some important dimension (Aumann 1985; Binmore 1990). Using language very similar to the model-based view, Binmore writes, "The sensible question to ask of a classification system is therefore not so much whether it can be said to be 'true or untrue' but whether it works. In this it resembles an office filing system or a complex computer program more than a 'scientific' theory" (31–32). For instance, Cox (1990) develops a model that allows us to classify electoral systems by five characteristics: district magnitude, electoral formula, number of votes each voter is allowed to cast, whether voters can cumulate their votes, and whether voters can choose to abstain partially. This model "works" because it helps us distill voting systems into their essential elements.

Richard F. Fenno's (1978) classic work on congressional districts, which also fits into this category, begins with the question, "What does a House member see when looking at his or her constituency?" (1). He goes on to argue for viewing constituents as being located within nested concentric circles, with a personal constituency of intimates at the core, moving out to a primary constituency, a reelection constituency, and finally, a geographic constituency. Fenno makes no claim that his is the correct or most accurate way of undertaking such a classification. Rather, he uses the language of helpfulness, arguing that "there can be no one 'correct' way of slicing up and classifying member perceptions—only 'helpful' ways," and suggesting that his concentric circles approach has been the most useful for his purposes (1). Fenno's categorization has shaped studies of Congress since its publication.

4.3.3 Exploratory Models

Models serve an exploratory function when used to investigate the putative (causal) mechanisms or motivations underlying phenomena of interest (Little 1991). Black notes that the "memorable models of science are 'speculative instruments'" (1962, 237). "Speculation" comes in several forms. Researchers may want to examine the impact of x on y, where x and y can take on any number of forms. For instance, x may be a legislative rule and y the resulting behavior of legislators or a policy outcome. In some cases, unexpected or counterintuitive findings result from such an exploration.

Romer and Rosenthal (1978), for example, model a revenue-maximizing agenda setter proposing a budget to voters. If the voters approve the budget, it is enacted. If the voters fail to approve the budget, a reversion budget automatically goes into effect. The counterintuitive result is that the more austere the reversion budget, the more power the agenda setter has. The reasoning is simple. For austere reversion budgets (those budgets that are lower than either the median voter or the agenda setter would like), there is an inverse relationship between the size of the reversion budget and the budget that is ultimately enacted. That is, the more severe the reversion budget, the greater government spending, and the better off the agenda setter is. The intuition that an agency head should be more fearful of an austere reversion budget than a generous budget is incorrect, provided the agency head is the agenda setter.

Exploratory models also allow the researcher to examine the impact of institutions, rules, or other constraints on behavior. For example, Moe (1989) constructs a verbal rational choice model of how bureaucracies are designed, often to fail, and shows how the model is helpful for understanding the creation of agencies like the Consumer Product Safety Commission. Moe assumes that the politics of agency creation has two main features: uncertainty and compromise. The nature of the uncertainty lies in the fact that administrations will come and go, and so will leadership in an agency. Rational actors, then, will not want to give an agency enough leeway so that it can, under different leaders, take policy in a direction very different than what its creators wanted. Compromise relates to the competing interests involved in agency creation, all of whom wish to have the agency do their bidding. The result of this uncertainty and compromise, Moe argues, is layer upon layer of rules and restrictions that hamstring the agency's effectiveness. This inertia is not an accident but is the product of rational action on the part of special interests and members of Congress responding to those interests.

As we noted earlier in the chapter, models used in this way prove useful both for positive and normative analyses of political phenomenon. Exploratory models, combined with normative criteria, are used to establish the desirability of particular institutional configurations. Suppose that a criterion were as follows: prefer electoral systems that create incentives for legislators to provide public goods benefiting all citizens versus providing redistribution or other targeted benefits. Theoretical models of legislative bargaining under different electoral systems provide one way to assess whether an electoral system is likely to satisfy this criterion.

One can also design exploratory models with an eye toward explaining the events surrounding a specific case or small number of cases, or to ask and answer counterfactual or "what if" questions regarding events such as the Cuban missile crisis (Lebow and Stein 1996).[10] An excellent example is Epstein and Knight (2002), who use two game theoretic models to analyze the conflict between Thomas Jefferson and John Marshall over judicial review: "By varying the relevant conditions in the game, we can assess the relative merits of the historical counterfactuals that underlie the different explanations of this period" (48).

Bates et al. (1998) propose the idea of analytic narratives as a way of explaining particular events and outcomes through the use of models. A narrative proceeds by first detailing the actors involved in the event, their motivations, their actions, and the resulting outcomes. One then constructs a model (or models) offering an account of the event by abstracting away from some details and zeroing in on certain mechanisms or features of the strategic environment. The authors propose to use this method to explain events such as the U.S. Civil War and the development of the international coffee trade.

Scholars disagree about whether models *ought* to be used for the purpose of studying lone events. It may seem that there is little to be gained from using models to understand a single event. After all, several different models may be written down that "fit the data." The key question is whether the exploratory model helps one make sense of the facts of the case and the decisions made by actors at key points in the development of the case. That is one purpose of an exploratory model. To criticize such models because they deal with discrete events and do not generalize is to criticize exploratory models for not being something they are not meant to be.[11]

4.3.4 Predictive Models

Prediction is the function of models with which we are most familiar, although actual examples of *theoretical* models whose main purpose is prediction are quite rare. Rather, most theoretical models of this sort are focused on *postdiction* or *retrodiction*, making predictions about the past, in the form of H-D and/or falsificationism. In other words, the purpose of the model is to generate testable hypotheses that can then be used in statistical tests on existing data, with the goal of informing us about the theoretical model. We have discussed the problems with this approach at length in chapter 2, and we discuss combining theoretical models and models of data in chapter 6, so we do not describe these types of models any further at this point.

4.4 JUDGING A THEORETICAL MODEL

4.4.1 Prediction Is the Wrong Standard (Usually)

Prediction is often seen as the "crucial activity" in science, and models are often judged by how well they predict (Brady 2004b). One of the world's leading economists, David Kreps, writes that the "purpose of game theory is to help economists understand and predict what will happen in economic contexts," and he takes as given that "improvement in understanding by itself implies improvement in predictions" (Kreps 1990, 5, 6). Yet in delineating the successes of game theory for economic analysis, he discusses four accomplishments:

- a taxonomy for economic situations through strategic form games such as the Prisoner's Dilemma;
- a language for modeling dynamic competitive interactions through extensive form games;
- an understanding of when threats are credible;
- a framework for understanding the role of information in shaping strategic interactions. (Kreps 1990, ch. 4)

As one reads Kreps's description of these successes, it becomes clear that *prediction* is not the reason these accomplishments are noteworthy. Kreps, for instance, points to the Prisoner's Dilemma (PD) as an example of a successful model. In its basic form, the PD predicts that defection should always occur in any finitely repeated version of the game. Yet in experimental settings, players cooperate at least some of the time (Dawes and Thaler 1988). Sally (1995), in a meta-analysis of the experimental literature utilizing more than 100 studies from 1958 to 1992, finds that the mean level of cooperation within each study is around 50 percent. Different arguments have been made for why this occurs. Selten and Stoecker (1986) claim that as players gain experience with the game, defection becomes more common. Researchers have modified the PD to account for incomplete information about player types (Kreps et al. 1982), and the modification has led to research examining whether altruism or reputation building encourages cooperation. Even so, behavior in experiments is still mixed with respect to the modified models' predictions (Andreoni and Miller 1993; Cooper et al. 1996). It surely cannot be the case that the value of the PD lies in its predictive ability.[12] Nevertheless, this does not stop leading figures in experimental economics from focusing on falsification with respect to the PD and related games. In contrast, Camerer (2003, 46), after pointing out how players deviate from the equilibrium prediction of these games, is careful to point out that cooperative behavior in collective action settings does not "falsify" game theory. His reasoning is that there is uncertainty regarding how different players value money and about how "other-regarding" players are.

Similarly, a leading political scientist, Morris Fiorina (1975), writes that clearly all models distort reality to one degree or another, and modelers should not believe that their model is *the* explanation, only that it is one of many." Fiorina then expresses mixed feelings about Milton Friedman's (1953) emphasis on prediction as the basis for theory evaluation. When discussing the uses of theoretical models, Fiorina focuses on models that are designed to explain known regularities (organizational models) and models that consider alternative institutional arrangements (exploratory models).

One of the great strengths of the model-based approach is that it allows us to go beyond prediction and judge whether a model is useful for a variety of purposes. Consider the legion of models that have proven enormously useful in furthering the discipline despite their lack of predictive accuracy. The spatial model, first employed in an electoral setting by Downs (1957), is a case in point. The model predicts that the optimal policy stance in two-party competition is for both parties to locate at the ideal point of the median voter. This result is clearly not borne out empirically; candidates take different policy stances, typically away from the median. Despite this lack of predictive accuracy, the model has been extraordinarily fruitful in providing intuition into candidate competition. In fact, many other applications of the spatial model similarly make predictions that are not accurate. Complete information spatial models of interbranch and legislative bargaining predict that blocking devices such as filibusters and vetoes should not occur, and yet, of course, they do (Krehbiel 1998). These models are still useful because they help us study the threat value of blocking techniques.

Moreover, it is sometimes necessary to write down models that produce outcomes that are at odds with empirical experience in order to better understand that experience. A complete information model showing that wars are inefficient and should never occur points to the role of incomplete or asymmetric information in shaping interactions among countries; this same logic is true for labor strikes. Riker and Ordeshook's (1968) seminal model showing that voting is not instrumentally rational led naturally to the question, "Given that voting is not instrumentally rational, why do people vote?" as well as the question, "What features, when added to a formal model of turnout, render voting instrumentally rational?"

Hinich and Munger (1997, 5) view this progression in quasi-falsificationist terms: "Without careful empirical tests, models would just be amusing mathematical exercises. Analytical political theory has been subjected to extensive and rigorous empirical testing. Partly because some portions of the theory ... *failed* empirical tests, the theory itself has evolved and been improved." But to say that the above models "predict poorly" or are not "empirically supported" is to miss (what should be) the point of these exercises, which is to serve as a starting point for further analysis.

Even when their models are fulfilling other purposes, researchers often return to the idea of falsificationism or model testing. Bates et al. (2000), defending their analytic narratives approach from a critique by Elster (2000), write,

> First, we model a portion of the critical dynamics in a way that affords tests of parts of the idea. This in itself is worthwhile. Second, we go farther and attempt to use the single case to generate hypotheses applicable to a larger set of cases. It is only in developing the account or model that we are pushed toward seeing what components of the account are testable . . . (697)

They go on to write, "We believe that rational choice offers a superior approach because it generates propositions that are refutable. Being subject to standard methods of evaluation—such as the out-of-sample testing of predictions and the systematic pursuit of falsification—the models we employ are not mere just-so stories" (700).[13] Their defense is defensible, at least given the rhetoric of their opponents, but it should be unnecessary and misses what is fruitful about analytic narratives. In another critique of their work, Carpenter (2000, 658) asks, "How does one 'test' an analytic narrative, or, better yet, how does one use narrative to test a theory?" However, the "testability" of the model used to explain the narrative is simply irrelevant. That testability is nevertheless one of the criteria for judging the narratives approach shows how problematic our reliance on falsificationism and H-D really is.

The instinct to revert back to falsificationism when defending one's model or approach is problematic for two reasons. First, the focus on model acceptance and rejection prevents us from viewing models as tools for exploration, hindering model development. We all start our research with some goals in mind. To the extent that we focus on model testing, we may construct our models differently, ignore potentially interesting modeling alternatives, and therefore move away from our original purpose in designing the model. Naturally, it is hard to quantify or measure the scientific harm caused by the emphasis on H-D, but we believe the effect to be large and real.

Second, the current focus of rational choice scholars on prediction and testability provides ammunition for critics, who use the lack of predictive accuracy of rational choice models as a cudgel. Much of Green and Shapiro's (1995) critique of rational choice models hinges on prediction and a falsificationist or perhaps Lakatosian view of the world, their protestations to the contrary. (They also have a very narrow view of what a model is, ruling out many important contributions because they "contain no theorems, no game-theoretic models, and no formal exposition of any kind"; see Green and Shapiro 1995, 244.) Initially, critics of the book focused on the many other uses of models, on how rational choice certainly merits its place in science in a Lakatosian view of the world, and on the limitations of quantitative "tests" of models, most notably in a special issue of the journal *Critical Review* (e.g., Diermeier 1995; Ferejohn and Satz 1995; Fiorina 1995; Shepsle 1995; but see Chong 1995, 47, for a discussion of falsifiability as a "virtue" of a theory). In recent years, though, the idea that "testable" models are superior to models that are not testable has become common, as chapter 2 makes clear. Green and Shapiro, like many others, mistake a lack of predictive accuracy for a lack of usefulness. To the extent that scholars refer to their models as superior or better because they are "testable" or "falsifiable," and to the extent that the EITM movement argues that testability is the primary metric by which to judge theoretical models (e.g., Aldrich and Alt 2003, 309), Green and Shapiro seem to have defined the terms of the debate. This outcome is, to say the least, unfortunate.

4.4.2 The Illusion of Precise Standards

Clearly, an elucidation of some standards is necessary for evaluating theoretical models. Models may be used for myriad purposes, so predictive success cannot be (as it too often is) the only metric by which we assess models. Prediction may, in fact, be orthogonal to a model's goals. Given that models are purpose-relative (Morton 1993), proper evaluation must begin by asking whether the model achieves the author's stated purpose (or fulfills a purpose perhaps unanticipated by the researcher, as when a model becomes foundational). A model's purpose generates its own metric of success.

The metric of success, however, cannot realistically be as precise as researchers might like. Even seemingly precise standards, such as the 0.05 p-value that is the gold standard in empirical work, are arbitrary, but nonetheless exert a powerful force. Achen (1982, 45) calls for a focus on substantive significance instead of statistical significance, but notes that this measure is of subjective value, especially compared to the "automated testing with sanctified 5% significance levels." He defends this approach in a way that applies equally to our argument: "There are no real benefits in clinging to routinized answers to irrelevant questions just to avoid giving less mechanical replies to the queries that matter" (45).

This norm has real consequences for scientific progress, as there is ample evidence that an emphasis on this 0.05 significance level biases the results that are published. Gerber and Malhotra (2008a) show that the top journals in political science tend to publish a disproportionate number of findings with Z-statistics at or around 1.96 for two-tailed tests and 1.84 for one-tailed tests.[14] These, of course, are the precise values that correspond to p-values of 0.05. Gerber and Malhotra point out that their results are consistent with findings in other disciplines, like medicine and economics. Although these authors do not statistically examine the source of this bias, they propose two related possibilities: one, editors and referees fixate on the 0.05 threshold when evaluating articles, and two, researchers may massage their data analyses or present selected specifications that give results just meeting that threshold. One implication of this bias is that many literatures may have overly optimistic views of effect sizes, with this effect being especially pronounced for small samples (Gerber, Green, and Nickerson 2001).

The statistical significance problem is partly due to a focus on a particular cutoff in an otherwise continuous significance test (with p-values ranging from 0 to 1). In some ways, the focus on generating "testable hypotheses" as a marker of a good model is a similar litmus test in the world of theoretical models. We reject this emphasis. Models ought to be judged by whether they fulfill a specific purpose. For reasons we hope this book makes clear, there is no reason that models generating testable hypotheses ought to be more highly valued than those that do not.

So are there ways to determine whether a model fulfills its purpose, or whether model A is "better" than model B in fulfilling a particular purpose? (We hold a discussion of empirical models for chapters 5 and 6.) Certainly researchers have tried. For instance, Bates et al. (1998) pose five questions to ask when evaluating an analytic narrative:

- Do the assumptions fit the facts, as they are known?
- Do conclusions follow from premises?
- Do its implications find confirmation in the data?
- How well does the theory stand up by comparison with other explanations?
- How general is the explanation? Does it apply to other cases?

We applaud the authors for stating their evaluative methods clearly, but we take issue with these being the metric for evaluating an exploratory model (of which a rigorous analytic narrative is an example). Taking the questions in order, researchers may have all sorts of reasons for using assumptions they know to be false, even when constructing a "narrative." As we discuss in chapter 3, to build a model requires us to focus on some features of the world and ignore others. Focusing on the accuracy of assumptions opens the door for critics to play the "unrealistic assumptions" card (Elster 2000). The second question is a standard for all deductive models, but this criterion really amounts to a basic logical consistency test. The third question is simply inappropriate for the purpose being discussed. If the goal is to construct a model that helps us understand a particular case or event, then our goal is *the construction of a model that matches the data*. If that is so, then the narrative, to the extent that it is complete, will answer this question in the affirmative. Bates et al. here revert back to falsificationism:

Initially the theory is formed from the data; it is selected because
it appears to offer a good fit. Rendered explicit, the theory then
becomes vulnerable; it can be subject both to logical appraisal
and to empirical testing. Its logic, moreover, renders it as a source
of insights, leading to the gathering of new data and placing
the theory at further risk. The richer the theory, the greater the
number of testable implications, and thus the greater the risk of
being found wanting.

(Bates et al. 1998, 17)

Oddly, Bates et al. abandon falsificationism in their discussion of
the fourth question. They write that falsificationism does not help us
adjudicate among theories or models and point the reader toward
theories that can explain more or reconcile competing alternatives.
Their final question, about generalizability, seems out of place if the
goal is to use a model to explore why a particular event materialized.

4.4.3 Dimensions of Usefulness

Rather than purport to having found some magic bullet for judging
models, we instead present questions to ask of one's model, depending
on its purpose. There are two dimensions on which to judge a model,
given its purpose, to assess its usefulness. The first is fecundity. That
is, does the model produce a series of important insights or just one?
Every political scientist can think of examples that may qualify as
"tweaked" models, making one small change to an existing model to
produce a new insight of little importance. These models are generally
not as valued as those that move in completely new directions, or
build on an existing theoretical framework but develop several new
insights.

Second, how important are the insights? A model with just one
insight—if it is important enough—may be more valuable than a
model that produces several vapid results. Similarly, a new sort of
model that can be adapted to many different strategic environments
should be valued, even if its initial incarnation does not produce

a litany of results. It is difficult to quantify the marginal rate of substitution for fecundity versus significance. But again, quantification for quantification's sake is not our goal. As legal scholar Lewis Kornhauser (2009, 3) argues: "A likely answer ... to the question: 'are models of type A better models of adjudication than models of type B?' is thus likely to be no. Sometimes type A models will be the appropriate ones, and sometimes type B models will be. We must evaluate models in terms of their fitness for their intended use." The following questions are presented in this spirit.

> *Foundational*: How flexible is the model? Can it be adapted to many different situations? Does the model cause scholars to overhaul an existing line of inquiry or move in entirely new directions?
>
> *Organizational*: Does the model subsume a large set of models, or a perhaps smaller set of seminal or important models? Alternatively, does the model subsume a large set of empirical generalizations or facts, or perhaps unify a small number of previously puzzling empirical findings? If a classification system, does the classification system help us better understand how cases are connected?
>
> *Exploratory*: Does the model generate a significant number of interesting statements or probe counterfactuals in new ways? Does the model lead the researcher to examine data in new ways?

We appreciate that our refusal to provide "cookbook" answers to theoretical model evaluation runs the risk of sounding like an "anything goes" approach. If there are no firm metrics for evaluating a model, how can we assert that one model is superior to another, or that one family of models is superior to another? We argue that researchers already make such determinations. Models generating uninteresting or narrow results wither on the vine; there is a reason why many modeling papers generate little more than a smattering of citations. The key is that the right mindset is used to judge models. Our concern about political science today is that all models, regardless of their purpose, are increasingly being judged on the basis of "testability" rather than usefulness.

Another advantage of our approach to model evaluation is that it allows models to be complementary as well as competing. In popular views of science we reject theories or models when their predictions are false, whereas in reality competing theories often remain to fight another day. This is true even in "real" sciences like physics. Cartwright (1983, 17) avers, "There is no single explanation which is the right one, even in the limit, or relative to the information at hand. Theoretical explanation is, by its very nature, redundant. This is one of the endemic features of explanation in physics which the deductive-nomological (D-N) account misses." Morrison (2005, 169) takes a similar view: "The successful use of models does not involve refinements to a unique idealized representation of a some phenomenon or group of properties, but rather a proliferation of structures, each of which is used for different purposes." Aumann (1985, 8–9) relays a story that is worth reprinting:

> It is even possible for two competing theories to exist happily side by side and be used simultaneously, in much the same way that many of us file letters both chronologically and by the name of the correspondent. Two famous examples are relativistic vs Newtonian mechanics, and wave vs particle theories of light. In each case each of the theories has its areas of usefulness. I remember reading in my teens that one famous scientist considered the wave theory "true" on Mondays, Wednesdays and Fridays, whereas he preferred the particle theory on Tuesdays, Thursdays and Saturdays (apparently he didn't work on Sundays). He used either, at convenience, on any day of the week; but the problem of which one was "true" seems [not] to have bothered him. Apparently he didn't subscribe to my view of science; or maybe his flippant remark was meant to indicate that he did, that the matter of "truth" was secondary to him, and that the most important thing was to get on with his work.[15]

4.5 CONCLUSION

We close this chapter with a passage from Laver (1997, 7) that nicely captures the essence of our argument:

> In the end, the criteria we in practice use to evaluate the usefulness of a model are very subjective, and this is in somewhat paradoxical contrast to the apparent rigour of the models themselves. In the real world people take up and use models they like and find useful, as long as these have no glaring logical errors. They ignore models that they don't like or find useless, despite the fact that these may be awesome logical constructions. This is as it should be, for a model of the political world is no more than a tool to help us expand our understanding. And we use those tools that we find useful, leaving on the shelf those that we do not. Your choice of which model to use for a particular job is, provided the model you choose is not inherently faulty, ultimately a matter of taste.[16]

Ultimately, the peer review process in science determines which models are useful and which ones are not. Of course, this state of affairs can be problematic to the extent that the focus is on one sort of analysis (H-D), but as we hope this chapter shows, scholars have the correct instincts that models ought to be used for purposes other than prediction. Once we can overcome the H-D hurdle we identify in this book, we are confident that these other ways models can be useful will become more common, and researchers who clearly have other purposes in mind will no longer have to defend their models on H-D terms.

Empirical Models

I have no patience with social scientists, historians, and philosophers who insist that the "scientific method" is doing experiments to check somebody's theory. The best physics I have known was done by experimenters who ignored theorists completely and used their own intuitions to explore new domains where no one had looked before. No theorists had told them where and how to look.

—Theoretical particle physicist HARRY LIPKIN

5.1 INTRODUCTION

We began chapter 3 by noting that political scientists use the term "model" in many ways. There are game theoretic models, formal models, computational models, verbal models, and empirical or statistical models. We discussed game theoretic and formal models in the last chapter under the rubric of theoretical models. Here we discuss empirical or statistical models, which are more prevalent in the literature than game theoretic models, computational models, or verbal models. There are statistical models of the democratic peace (Maoz and Russett 1993), of the ideal points of members of Congress (Poole and Rosenthal 1985; Clinton, Jackman, and Rivers 2004), of judicial decision making in Argentina (Helmke 2005), and of the causal effect of terrorism on Israeli voters (Berrebi and Klor 2008).

Empirical models in political science are most often used to "test" theoretical models, whether formal or verbal. This use is in keeping with the field's belief that theoretical models must be tested. It is not a coincidence that theoretical particle physicist Harry Lipkin singles out social scientists in this chapter's epigraph. Although Lipkin's views are not without controversy (see the letters that follow in the January 2001 issue of *Physics Today*, as well as Lipkin's reply), his statements show that even in the hard sciences there is little agreement on a scientific method, never mind one that insists that empirical models be used to check theoretical models.[1] In chapter 4, we took issue with the claim that theoretical models must be tested and demonstrated how they may be useful without undergoing testing. In this chapter, we argue that empirical models may be useful even when not tied to a theoretical model.

Some view the distinction we make between theoretical and statistical models as unnecessary. In one sense, they are all models, and empirical models, like theoretical models, should be viewed as objects that are neither true nor false. Empirical models have limited accuracy, are partial, and are purpose-relative. Like theoretical models, empirical models are constructed for specific reasons. In another sense, however, empirical models and theoretical models are quite distinct. The key difference is that an empirical model, regardless of its other uses, should describe accurately the dependencies within a given data set. Empirical models therefore cannot attain the same level of generality that theoretical models do because where theory is general, data are specific, tied to particular places and times.[2] Thus, empirical models are yoked to the phenomenological world in ways that theoretical models are not. One way this difference manifests itself is that empirical models often must contain variables that do not appear in their theoretical counterparts. These additional variables, in effect, perform the same function that *ceteris paribus* clauses do in theoretical models.[3] A second way the difference between theoretical and empirical models manifests itself is that empirical models need to undergo rigorous assumption testing to establish the empirical adequacy of the model (more on this later). Theoretical models need not undergo similar testing to establish their adequacy, which stems from the internal logic of the model and the interests of the modeler.

Of course, theoretical and empirical models differ in other ways as well. An empirical model produces results in conjunction with data and the state of statistical science.[4] The success of an empirical model, therefore, relies on factors that often remain beyond the control of the modeler. No empirical model, for example, is worth anything without quality data. The problems associated with measurement error and missing data are often severe enough to distort the conclusions from any empirical model, no matter how good. Empirical models also rely on auxiliary machinery in a way that theoretical models do not. The properties of many common estimators are known only asymptotically, and a researcher can never be sure exactly when asymptotic results apply. Empirical models can fail in ways that theoretical models cannot, and it makes sense to treat these different models separately.

In what follows, we define the term *empirical model* and note the nature of its construction. Because empirical models are purpose-relative, we address the various uses to which they may be put. We focus in particular on theory testing and demonstrate that pairing an empirical model with a theoretical model does not constitute a test of the theoretical model. The problem lies in the deductive connection between the theory and the hypothesis, as discussed in chapter 2, and the deductive connection between the hypothesis and the data as filtered through the empirical model. Lest anyone conclude from this demonstration that empirical models are not useful or are unscientific, we end the chapter with examples of empirical models, drawn from the political science literature, which were constructed for purposes other than theory testing.

5.2 WHAT IS AN EMPIRICAL MODEL?

Empirical models in political science vary enormously both in the complexity of the techniques needed to estimate them and in the restrictiveness of their assumptions (although assumptions and techniques are not mutually exclusive categories). The variety of modeling techniques available to political scientists ranges from correlations, which assume a simple linear model (Hanushek and

Jackson 1977), to the familiar classical linear regression model
(Greene 2003), to nonlinear panel models estimated by the method
of simulated moments (Cameron and Trivedi 2005). The restrictiveness of the available models ranges from parametric models
to semiparametric models to nonparametric and distribution-free
models (Mittlehammer, Judge, and Miller 2000). However, despite
the proliferation of empirical models in the discipline, most political
scientists would be hard pressed to express exactly what these models
have in common. What is needed is a common language for describing
and categorizing empirical models.

If we were to ask a mainstream statistician to define "statistical
model," the answer might come back that a statistical model is a "set
of probability distributions on the sample space S" (McCullagh 2002,
1225). Another statistician might say that a model is just "a subset
of the statistics space" (de Leeuw 1994).[5] Neither definition is likely
to mean much to a political scientist, who is accustomed to thinking
about empirical models either in terms of substantive theory (the
onset of a militarized interstate dispute is a function of the balance
of forces, etc.) or in terms of statistical technique ("I ran a Bayesian
hierarchical linear model"). An empirical model in political science,
however, is neither simply a set of probability distributions nor simply
a statistical technique. What is missing from these definitions is the
actual political science; there is no explicit room for substance. On the
other hand, empirical models are also more than substance; they are
not just theoretical models with error terms.

A more helpful definition comes from Spanos (1999), who
decomposes a statistical model into three components: a probability
model, a sampling model, and a statistical generating mechanism.
The probability model corresponds to the statistical definition of a
model given in the last paragraph. It comprises a collection of density
functions along with a set of unknown parameters and the support
of the densities (Spanos 1999, 98).[6] The sampling model is a set
of random variables with a probabilistic structure.[7] It is through the
sampling model that the observed data is related to the probability
model. Substance enters the model through the statistical generating

mechanism, which provides "a bridge between the statistical model and the theoretical model" (Spanos 1999, 368).[8]

Consider the well-known classical linear regression model as an example. The statistical generating mechanism is

$$Y_i = \beta_0 + \beta_1 x_i + \epsilon_i,$$

where the disturbances, ϵ_i, have mean 0 and variance σ^2. The probability model is the Normal distribution conditioned on the right-hand-side variables with parameters β and σ^2.[9] The sampling model $(Y_1, Y_2, \ldots, Y_n)$ is an independent sample (Spanos 1999, 373).

What Spanos's tripartite definition highlights is the fact that a statistical model is not simply a theoretical model with an appended error term. Rather, a statistical model incorporates both theoretical information and statistical information, and much of the statistical information must come from the data being modeled. The data contain information pertinent to the probability model and the sampling model, such as independence, heterogeneity, and the probability distribution, that the theoretical model often does not (and perhaps should not in the interests of parsimony). The importance of this sample information lies in the realization that the process of learning from an empirical model is partially deductive (Spanos 1999, 560). That is, the soundness of any conclusion a researcher draws from his or her statistical model depends completely on the appropriateness of the assumptions being made. For example, many of the conclusions a researcher might draw from a statistical model are premised on the absence of non-negligible measurement error. The deductive argument is that if the variables are measured without error, then the inferential results will hold, *ceteris paribus*. If the premise of that argument is not true, the inferential results are unlikely to hold, as nearly all the desirable properties of an estimator in classical statistics are destroyed by nonrandom measurement error. It is this deductive aspect of statistical arguments that leads to the phrase heard by first-year graduate students (Spanos mentions it as well): garbage in, garbage out.

Whatever other uses political scientists have for empirical models, the first goal of empirical modeling must be statistical adequacy. If the model is not statistically adequate, that is, the assumptions of the model are a poor match to reality, no valid conclusions can be drawn. Assumption testing, therefore, is a crucial aspect of any empirical modeling project, whereas it is a decidedly unimportant part of a theoretical modeling project.[10] In constructing an empirical model, a researcher must go beyond the theoretical model and pay attention to the data.

The argument just made does not mean that theoretical models cannot inform our understanding of data (and vice versa). It could be argued that all empirical models are constructed from mental models, for lack of a better term, that exist only in our minds. When constructing an empirical model of the effect of democracy on the war-proneness of states, we control for wealth instead of flag color because of that mental model. More formally, theoretical models are an invaluable aid to empirical modeling when questions of identification arise. The clearest example involves simultaneous equations, where identification concerns the ability to recover estimates of the structural coefficients from reduced-form coefficients. Ensuring that a system of equations is identified requires the use of *a priori* nonsample information that cannot be deduced from the data and generally must come from a theoretical model. These points should be kept in mind as we discuss the relationship between theoretical and empirical models.

5.2.1 A Model-Based Understanding

The definition that we offer of a statistical model underscores the importance of the model-based approach. Indeed, Spanos (1999, 544) argues that statistical models are not linguistic entities and argues for a semantic conception of models. In chapter 3, we introduced the model-based approach, which views models as tools or instruments—in particular, as maps. We demonstrated, with the help of a few examples, that theoretical models, like maps, are neither true nor false, have limited accuracy, are partial, and are purpose-relative.

Statistical models are maps in precisely the same sense that theoretical models are maps, and statistical models share many of the same map-like characteristics as theoretical models. No matter how complicated or arcane the empirical model, the difference between empirical models and theoretical models is that the former map, or characterize, the relationship between two or more variables in a data set. Consider the classical linear regression model already introduced,

$$y_i = \beta_0 + \beta_1 x_i + \epsilon_i, \ \epsilon_i \sim \text{IID} \, N(0, \sigma^2),$$

where y_i is one of n observations on the dependent variable, x_i is one of n observations on the explanatory variable, β_0 and β_1 are unknown coefficients, and ϵ_i is one of n disturbances. The model assumes that the disturbances are drawn from Normal distributions with the same mean and the same variance, and that the value of any particular disturbance is uncorrelated with the value of any other disturbance.

Let us consider the various components of the map analogy in relationship to the linear regression model. First, the model is an object and thus neither true nor false. Statistician Jan de Leeuw writes,

> We must immediately take issue with the idea that the model is, in some sense, "true." This notion is difficult to define, and largely irrelevant. The definitions given so far lead us to conclude that, if the word means anything, then models are most certainly *not* true . . . Models can be extremely *useful* and *efficient*, even though they are obviously untrue.
>
> (de Leeuw 1994, 144)[11]

The model describes a hypothetical relationship between a variable x and a variable y. The model exists and is a tool that we can use to analyze data. The question is whether this tool is useful in describing an actual relationship between a real x and a real y. Second, the model has limited accuracy. The fit of the model to any particular x and y will not be perfectly accurate; few of the data points in a regression analysis of actual data lie directly on the regression line. The line is a summary of a relationship (the model replaces the actual data points with an estimate of the conditional mean of y for each value of x), and like most summaries, information is lost. Third, the model is partial. Other variables that may be related both to x and y are omitted from the specification.[12] Finally, the model is purpose-relative. Whether the variables omitted from the specification cause a problem depends on the use to which the model is put. Theory testing may require a different specification from prediction. (In the next section, we detail the different uses for statistical models and assess how well statistical models fulfill those purposes.)

A complete understanding of the model-based approach to empirical models requires discussion of the theoretical hypotheses (if we are to follow Giere 1990 closely). As in the case of theoretical models, the relationship between a model and a real-world system is made by the theoretical hypotheses, which assert that certain sorts of real systems are among members of that class (van Fraassen 1989). That is, a theoretical hypothesis states that an object, a system known as a model, is similar in some respect and for some purpose to another object, a real-world system. In the case of empirical models, the theoretical hypotheses concern the assumptions of the model. The assumptions must be similar enough to the actual structure of the data for the model to fulfill the purpose for which it is intended. Prediction requires a tighter fit between the model's assumptions and the data than other possible uses (see the next section). Again, the assertion that the model's assumptions be "similar enough" is quite different from the assertion that the assumptions must be, in any sense, true. Many different probability distributions mirror one another over certain ranges or for certain parameter values, and a lack of independence may not be at issue if what a researcher cares about is solely the estimated coefficient.

The relationship between an empirical model and the data described by it is depicted in figure 5.1. An empirical model, M, is characterized by a probability distribution, Φ, a sampling model, $\mathbf{X}$, and a statistical generating mechanism, $G.M$. The goal of the empirical model is to describe the relationships between the variables in the data, $\mathbf{x}_i$, in

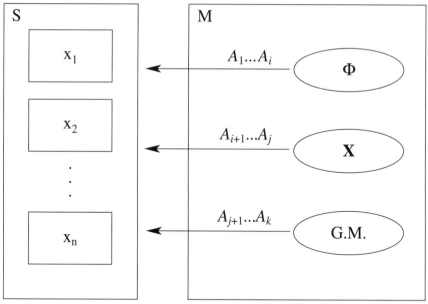

Figure 5.1 The Relationship between an Empirical Model, Its Assumptions, and the Data. *An empirical model, M, comprises a probability model Φ, a sampling model $\mathbf{X}$, and a statistical generating mechanism, G.M. These components are connected to the data, $\mathbf{x}_i$, in outcomes space, S, through assumptions, $A_1 \ldots A_k$.*

outcomes space, S. The choices made about the three components of the empirical model, that is, the assumptions, $A_1 \ldots A_k$, must adequately describe the data if the inferences from the model are to be worth anything.

5.3 THE PURPOSES OF EMPIRICAL MODELS

Just as there are many ways to categorize theoretical models, there are many ways to categorize empirical models. We could sort models by the statistical technique used to estimate them (maximum likelihood versus least squares versus minimum Chi-square), whether they are univariate or multivariate, inferential or descriptive, or causal or instrumental. The typology we use, in keeping with the theme of this volume, focuses on the *usefulness* of empirical models in political science.

Following Hoover (2006, 65–66), empirical models are used in one or more of four different roles: theory testing, prediction, measurement, and characterization.[13] Theory testing is both the use most familiar to political scientists and the use, we argue below, to which empirical models are least suited. The remaining three uses are conceptually distinct from theory testing, although they are most often used these days as an adjunct to theory testing.

Prediction is used in a number of different ways in political science. Some scholars, for example, use "prediction" to mean "comparative static" or "observed implication" (see Morton 1999). Others use "prediction" to mean postdiction, the prediction of events that have already occurred (Van Evera 1997, 28). Still others refer to "prediction" when they mean "forecasting," the prediction of future events. The first two uses of *prediction*, the use of comparative statics and postdiction, are closely associated with theory testing. The belief is that a "true" theory should be able to predict past events. Morton (1999, 102), for example, avers that "a model is not evaluated if its predictions are not analyzed." We address theory testing in the next section. Forecasting, on the other hand, is rarely the goal of empirical modeling in political science. A relatively recent report cataloged the frequencies of different methodological approaches in the top three political science journals and found forecasting accounted for only 9 percent of articles, not counting methods articles, political theory articles, and formal theory articles (Krueger and Lewis-Beck 2005, 19).[14]

The understanding of measurement has, in recent years, undergone a transformation from a truth-based view to a model-based view (Mari 2007). On the former account, measurement provides information that can be "interpreted in terms of reliability, certainty, accuracy, precision, etc." (62). Attention is paid to the two sources of error: systematic error (validity) and random error (reliability). The model-based account accepts that the measurability of a property depends on the current state of knowledge about the property as well as on the availability of experimental conditions (42). Thus, measurement is based on a model comprising "the available relevant knowledge on the object under measurement, the measuring system and the measurand" (65).

As with prediction, measurement has, of late, been less of a goal in and of itself, and more of a tool for theory testing.

Finally, an empirical model may be used to characterize the relationships within a data set. Berk (2004, 207), for example, offers the following ways characterization can be used in advocacy settings:

> Formal disputes often arise over what the facts really are. Were black employees less likely to be promoted than similarly situated white employees? Does the quality of water from various reservoirs in a city substantially differ? Does air quality vary in a city depending on the economic and racial mix of a neighborhood? Are there important salary differences between male and female faculty members at a particular university, once differences in department and rank are taken into account?

The point of these examples is that an empirical model can be useful without reliance on the more controversial aspects of empirical analysis: statistical and causal inference. In the final example just given, determining whether salary differences exist between male and female faculty members at a particular university does not require an inference to be made between a possibly nonrandom sample and a possibly ill-defined population, or an assumption that the data constitute a random draw from a superpopulation, or detailing a falsifiable causal theory of salaries that requires testing. Determining the answer to the question requires the specification of a statistically adequate empirical model that controls for the obvious sources of salary discrepancies.

Another way empirical models can be useful in the absence of theory testing is in spotting provocative associations that aid in later theory development or in the design of randomized experiments. Again, Berk (2004) notes that "virtually all" of the major randomized social experiments in recent memory—income subsidies for the poor, welfare reform, educational television, police interventions in domestic violence disputes, and many others—were informed by analyses that required no inference. The empirical models were useful nonetheless.

In political science, Achen (2002, 442) argues that two of the discipline's most robust quantitative generalizations, the democratic peace and the correlation between party identification and the vote, came from empirical modeling without the use of prior theory. Their existence is the result not of theory testing but of finding the correlations in a large number of studies. Both generalizations have generated large bodies of literature seeking to explain them.

Theory testing, however, lies at the heart of political *science* as we know it, and to theory testing we now turn.

5.4 THE ILLOGIC OF THEORY TESTING

Theory or model testing is far and away the use to which most empirical models are put. We provided some examples in chapter 2, but it cannot hurt to cite additional instances. As before, we restrict ourselves to well-regarded scholars publishing in well-regarded journals. Carpenter et al. (2010), for example, test their decision-theoretic model of dynamic product approval by an uncertain regulator using a duration analysis and data on new drug application approval times from 1950 to 2006. Carroll and Cox (2007) test their model of government formation, in which parties can form pre-election pacts, with a linear regression and data from parliamentary democracies from 1997 to 2005. Iversen and Soskice (2006) test their general model of redistribution using error correction models and panel data for redistribution, government partisanship, and electoral system in advanced democracies. Fowler (2005) tests his theory of dynamic responsiveness using a linear regression and a measure of legislative ideology. Shipan (2004) tests his theory of bureaucratic oversight with a linear regression and data on the monitoring activities of the U.S. Food and Drug Administration. Alvarez and Bedolla (2003) test their model of Latino voter partisanship with a multinomial logit and data from the 2000 Latino Voter Study. Mebane and Sekhon (2002) test their equilibrium model of turnout and vote choice decisions by midterm electors using maximum likelihood models and National Election Studies (NES) survey data. Clark and Hallerberg (2000) test their formal model of the interaction between fiscal and monetary policymakers using a pooled cross-sectional time-series model and data from the Organisation for Economic Co-operation and Development countries.

Some political scientists view theory testing as the point of using empirical models. Braumoeller and Sartori (2004, 144–45) write that "the most common underlying goal of research that uses statistics is to test and evaluate theories." The field agrees; today's modal political science journal article begins with a discussion of one or more theoretical models, which are then "tested" with an empirical model. A statement that the "data" support one or more of the theoretical models invariably follows.

Despite the rhetoric, few of the scholars cited here actually test their models in a logically consistent manner. Our critique of theory testing, however, should not be construed as inferring that the works just cited have no merit. Many of the publications make significant contributions on both the theoretical side and the empirical side. Our criticism concerns solely the claims made by these scholars regarding the extent to which their empirical models test their theoretical models. The problem lies in the logical connection between empirical and theoretical models.

In chapter 2, we addressed one set of problems generated by the use of hypothetico-deductivism (H-D). To summarize that argument, we noted that deductions are only truth preserving. We therefore have no expectation that a prediction derived from a model with false assumptions is true (or false). We also argued that determining the truth status of the observation sentences required by H-D is often quite difficult. Here we argue that these concerns are not ameliorated by the introduction of an empirical model. Our chief concern, however, is with the logical connection between the theoretical model and the empirical model. The difficulties of constructing a statistical model that accurately determines the state of the world are well documented elsewhere (see Lieberson 1985) and need not be repeated.

There are three general approaches to theory testing using empirical models being practiced by political scientists today: falsification-ism, verificationism, and Bayesian confirmation. Although political scientists often use the language of falsificationism (see, e.g., King, Keohane, and Verba 1994, 100–105) and some political scientists adopt a Bayesian approach to theory testing (Gill 2007), verificationism is the dominant model of theory testing in the discipline. Specifically, political scientists attempt to verify or confirm their theoretical models by pointing to an estimated coefficient of the "expected" size and direction. For strict falsificationists, testing a theoretical model in this fashion amounts to "playing tennis with the net down," and demonstrating that data conform to predictions is "replacing falsification, which is difficult, with verification, which is easy" (Blaug 1992, 241). The solution, according to Blaug and other avowed falsificationists, such as political scientists Green and Shapiro (1994), is to reestablish strict testing. In Green and Shapiro's case, this nostrum calls for the adoption of "sophisticated" falsificationism, in which a theory is corroborated only if it leads to the discovery of novel facts (182–183). In the following discussion, we cover all three modes of theory testing to demonstrate that pairing a theoretical model with an empirical model, regardless of the method of inference, cannot overcome the problems generated by H-D.

5.4.1 Falsificationism

We begin with falsificationism because political scientists (whether or not they actually practice it to the satisfaction of Blaug and others) often talk in terms of falsificationism. In addition, as we pointed out in chapter 2, classical hypothesis testing is based on the idea of falsificationism.

According to strict falsificationism, a theoretical model gains confirmation by surviving multiple attempts to falsify it (Chalmers 1982, 45). Our discussion, therefore, takes place in two parts. First, we show what falsificationists know to be true: that model confirmation is logically impossible under an H-D framework. Second, we show that falsification itself is impossible under the same framework.

We can represent attempts to confirm a theoretical model under falsificationism using the notation introduced in chapter 2. As a brief

(1) $TM \rightarrow \neg H_0$

(2) $\left.\begin{array}{l} H_0 \rightarrow P(y|H_0) \text{ is large,} \\ \quad P(y|H_0) \text{ is small} \end{array}\right\} \vdash \neg H_0$

(3) $\left.\begin{array}{l} TM \rightarrow \neg H_0 \\ \quad \neg H_0 \end{array}\right\} \not\vdash TM$

Figure 5.2 Unjustified Confirmation

recap, $\rightarrow$ means "if, then," $\neg$ stands for "not," $\vdash$ means "can validly conclude," $\not\vdash$ means "cannot validly conclude," H_0 stands for the null hypothesis, and $P(y|H_0)$ is the probability of the data given the null hypothesis. We let TM stand for the theoretical model. Classical hypothesis testing concerns the null hypothesis; the logic of statistical falsificationism is in figure 5.2.

Figure 5.2 represents the argument that if the theoretical model TM is true, then the null hypothesis H_0 must be false, and if the null hypothesis is false, then the theoretical model is confirmed. In (1), the theoretical model implies the falsity of the null hypothesis. In (2), the null hypothesis implies that the probability of seeing the data given the null hypothesis $P(y|H_0)$ is large. If the conditional probability is small, we can reject the null hypothesis in a normal application of Neyman-Pearson hypothesis testing.

Note, however, the double application of the H-D method. The first is between the theoretical model and the falsity of the null hypothesis, $TM \rightarrow \neg H_0$, and the second is found within the structure of classical hypothesis testing, $H_0 \rightarrow P(y|H_0)$ *is large.*[15]

The problem generated by the double application of H-D occurs in (3). Given that the null hypothesis is rejected, we cannot logically conclude that the theoretical model should be accepted. If we mistakenly draw this conclusion, we are guilty of the logical fallacy of affirming the consequent.[16] Consider, for example, a null hypothesis that states that the coefficient on a certain variable is zero, $H_0 : \beta = 0$.

Any theoretical model that includes the variable in question implies that this null hypothesis is false. Even if we were to restrict attention to plausible alternative theoretical models, there are far too many to allow confirmation of the model of interest. The falsity of the null hypothesis cannot serve as evidence for any one of these theoretical models.

Although model confirmation is not possible in this instance, it might be argued that something has been learned about the theoretical model in question from the rejection of the null hypothesis. This conclusion is unsatisfying for two reasons. First, there are few instances in political science where we believe that an effect is precisely zero, which is what the standard significance test assumes (Achen 1982, 45). Its rejection is usually unsurprising. Second, any confirmation of the theoretical model to be gleaned from such a test has force only if falsification is actually possible. We turn to this possibility next.

Figure 5.3 represents the argument that if the theoretical model is true, then the null hypothesis should be false, and if the null hypothesis is true, then the theoretical model is falsified. In (1), the theoretical model implies the falsity of the null hypothesis. In (2), the null hypothesis implies the probability of seeing the data given the null hypothesis $P(y|H_0)$ is large. If the conditional probability is large, we fail to reject the null hypothesis. Note that here we see again the logical fallacy of affirming the consequent. We fail to reject the null hypothesis that the variable has no effect, but in a classical framework, we cannot validly conclude that the null hypothesis is true. Assume for

$$(1)\ TM \rightarrow \neg H_0$$

$$(2)\ \left. \begin{array}{l} H_0 \rightarrow P(y|H_0) \text{ is large,} \\ P(y|H_0) \text{ is large} \end{array} \right\} \nvdash H_0$$

$$(3)\ \left. \begin{array}{l} T \rightarrow \neg H_0 \\ H_0 \end{array} \right\} \vdash \neg T$$

Figure 5.3 Unjustified Falsification

the moment that we fail to reject the null hypothesis because the confidence interval includes zero. As with any confidence interval, a number of values exist that may have led to this conclusion (all the values that lie inside the interval). No effect is only one of those values. To conclude on the basis that $P(y|H_0)$ is large that the variable has no effect is incorrect. (This reasoning explains why many political scientists are taught to say "fail to reject the null" instead of the affirmative "accept the null.") The logical mistake in (2) denies the falsification that occurs in (3). Failing to reject a null hypothesis cannot falsify the theoretical model in question. Thus, the researcher is faced with a situation in which she cannot either confirm or falsify the model under a strict falsificationist framework.

5.4.2 Verificationism

As noted earlier, strict falsification is not really what political scientists do. Despite all the ink spilled arguing for falsificationism, few political scientists actually try to falsify their theoretical models. Rather, they attempt to verify or confirm their theoretical models by asserting that an estimated coefficient of a certain size and direction "supports" or is "evidence in favor of" the hypothesis and therefore the theoretical model. Claims of this sort are antithetical to falsificationism, but they have come to dominate the actual practices of political scientists. Shipan (1996, 184), for example, writes, "the model performed as expected—all coefficients are in the predicted direction." Similarly, Lake and Baum (2001) hypothesize that democracies should produce larger quantities of public services. After running their analyses, the authors state that the results "strongly and consistently support" the hypothesis (609). They write that "as predicted by our primary hypothesis," the results indicate that "increases in democracy are, under varying conditions, significantly related to increases in the provision of public services" (613). There is no pretense of falsificationism here.

The standard practice, then, is to derive a research hypothesis, H_1, from a theoretical model, as opposed to deriving the falsity of the null

$$TM \rightarrow \left.\begin{array}{l} \text{Coefficient is correct,} \\ \text{Coefficient is correct} \end{array}\right\} \not\vdash TM$$

Figure 5.4 Verificationism in Reduced Form

hypothesis, H_0. The logic of verificationism begins with the derivation of H_1 from the model, $TM \rightarrow H_1$ ("if the theoretical model is true, then the research hypothesis is true"). The second deduction states that if the research hypothesis is true, then a certain statistical relation should hold in the data. We denote a claim of this sort as $H_1 \rightarrow$ *Coefficient is correct*, which reads, "If the research hypothesis is true, then the coefficient has the correct direction and size."

As the first deduction ends with H_1 ($TM \rightarrow H_1$) and the second begins with H_1 ($H_1 \rightarrow$ *Coefficient is correct*), we can represent the logic of verificationism in a reduced form in figure 5.4.

The argument in figure 5.4 is that if the theoretical model is true, then the coefficient should be correct in direction and size, and if the coefficient is correct in direction and size, then the theoretical model is correct. Once again, however, we see the fallacy of affirming the consequent. A coefficient that is the size and in the direction specified by a hypothesis cannot confirm the theoretical model that implied the hypothesis. As is always the case with logical fallacies in which we affirm the consequent, the same prediction may be a consequence of an infinite number of theoretical models. If an infinite number of models imply the same prediction, then no model is confirmed when the prediction is borne out.[17]

5.4.3 Bayesian Confirmation

Some political scientists have turned to Bayesianism in an attempt to avoid the problems of classical hypothesis testing.[18] In one formulation, Bayesianism is used in conjunction with the H-D method. A hypothesis is derived from theory, as normal, and then Bayesian methods are used to test it. Although this type of confirmation is one of the success stories of philosophical Bayesianism (Earman 1992, 63–65), it is of little use

$$TM \rightarrow P(H_1|y) \text{ is large,} \left.\begin{array}{c} \\ P(H_1|y) \text{ is large} \end{array}\right\} \not\vdash TM$$

Figure 5.5 Bayesian Confirmation

to the practical researcher interested in theory testing. The problem is once again the deductive structure of model confirmation in political science.

Figure 5.5 represents Bayesian confirmation. The Bayesian logic parallels the logic of the verificationist case with the Bayesian inverse probability statement, $P(H_1|y)$ *is large* (the probability of the research hypothesis given the data is high), replacing the statement that the *Coefficient is correct.*

As we can see in figure 5.5, the use of Bayesianism does not allow us to avoid the fallacy of affirming the consequent. Concluding *TM* on the basis that $P(H_1|y)$ *is large* is illogical because any theoretical model that implies the research hypothesis would also be confirmed. It is possible to conclude that the theoretical model is falsified if $P(H_1|y)$ *is small,* but as previously argued, political scientists are generally uninterested in falsifying their theories.[19] Moreover, falsificationism is inimical to mainstream Bayesian thought (Monari 1993).

We have demonstrated that the deductive connection between a theoretical model and an empirical model designed to test the theoretical model prevents any such testing from actually taking place. Empirical models, then, are of little use in theory testing. Avoiding this conclusion requires finding a connection between theoretical models and empirical models that eschews the fallacy of affirming the consequent. We delay this discussion until chapter 6.

5.5 THE OTHER USES OF EMPIRICAL MODELING

Although rare, political science articles do exist that feature empirical models that are not used to test theories. These uses can be categorized as prediction (in the forecasting sense), measurement, and characterization. A few of these models are used for multiple purposes.

The existence of these articles, which do not feature theoretical models used to deductively derive hypotheses or a pretense to modeling a data generating process, gives lie to the idea that these trappings are the *sine qua non* of science in political science.

In a 1991 article that was part of an influential research project, Keith Poole and Howard Rosenthal characterize the structure of congressional roll call voting. They argue that the structure is captured by a simple two-dimensional spatial model, in which each roll call is represented by two points (yea and nay), and a legislator votes for the alternative that he or she prefers. A legislator's preference for an alternative is captured by a simple utility function, where utility is decreasing in the distance between that alternative and a legislator's most preferred policy, known as his ideal point. The goal of this empirical model is purely instrumental; it is prediction, not explanation:

> We should stress that the work says nothing about how specific issues get defined in terms of the structure. We cannot, for example, explain why Robert Bork was rejected by the Senate ... we do show that it would have been possible, using our model, to have accurately predicted the Bork vote on the basis of announced positions by members of the Judiciary Committee. In other words, once the positions of the alternatives have been defined, a spatial model can predict the outcome.
>
> (Poole and Rosenthal 1991, 229)

The low-dimensional spatial model used by Poole and Rosenthal is a reflection not of a preexisting theoretical model but of careful and patient data analysis. The authors array seven sets of supporting evidence for it. They model interesting House sessions with additional dimensions and gauge the classification percentage. They look at how well both the first and second dimension do in classifying individually. They check whether different issues give different scales. They use more than one evaluation method (classification percentage and geometric mean probability). They consider the effect of issue diversity. Finally, they determine which issues actually lead to a second dimension. Poole and Rosenthal also consider the temporal stability of their model. They look to see if the model consistently fits the data in time, whether the first dimension is stable in time, and whether individual positions are stable in time. This level of data analysis is a far cry from what we normally see in political science, which is essentially the same model run over and over again with a variable dropped here and there.

Demonstrating where a model does not fit well is as important as demonstrating where it does fit, and to be useful, a model need not fit everywhere. Poole and Rosenthal present evidence that the one-dimensional spatial model does not fit well when the issues in question are slavery and civil rights for blacks. For the issue of slavery, destabilization occurred during the period when the Whigs were replaced by Republicans. For civil rights, the mid-1960s, when Southern Democrats separated themselves from Northern Democrats and there was a "virtual three-party system," is the period of worst fit (Poole and Rosenthal 1991, 261).

Poole and Rosenthal are after a model that predicts well. To be useful in this regard, no claims about the model's veracity need to be assessed. No hypotheses are explicitly derived from the model, and none are "tested." The authors present evidence that their model is useful, and they provide the reader with reasons for believing that this usefulness is not an accident. No inferences are made to vague populations, and no random samples are required. Nonetheless, few would argue with the scientific status of the Poole and Rosenthal project.

Very much the same thing can be said for the next example, which features a similar empirical model with a similar structure, but for a different primary purpose. In this instance, the central focus of the model is on measurement, as opposed to prediction.

Martin and Quinn (2002) set out to measure the policy preferences of U.S. Supreme Court justices. Their particular interest is whether those policy preferences change over time. The inquiry is prompted by the extensive use of estimated policy preferences as key explanatory variables in work by other scholars. If policy preferences are dynamic rather than static, the conclusions arrived at by previous work are suspect.

The analysis begins by deriving a dynamic item response model from a simple spatial model of voting. The spatial model specifies that justice j votes to reverse on case k when $z_{t,k,j} = \mu_{t,k,j}^{(r)} - \mu_{t,k,j}^{(a)} > 0$, where $\mu_{t,k,j}^{(r)}$ is the utility to justice j of voting to reverse on case k in term t, and $\mu_{t,k,j}^{(a)}$ is the utility to justice j of voting to affirm on case k in term t. The model is translated into a statistical model by assuming that for observed votes,

$$v_{t,k,j} = \begin{cases} 1 & \text{if } z_{t,k,j} > 0 \\ 0 & \text{if } z_{t,k,j} \leq 0, \end{cases}$$

where $z_{t,k,j} = \alpha_k + \beta_k \theta_{t,j} + \epsilon_{t,k,j}$, $\epsilon_{t,k,j} \overset{IID}{\sim} N(0, 1)$, and $\theta_{t,j}$ is justice j's ideal point in the unidimensional issue space for term t.

Letting α, β, and θ be the stacked versions of α_k, β_k, and θ_j, Bayesian inference for these parameters proceeds by summarizing the posterior density,

$$p(\alpha, \beta, \theta | V) \propto p(V | \alpha, \beta, \theta) p(\alpha, \beta, \theta),$$

where $p(\alpha, \beta, \theta)$ are prior beliefs and

$$p(V | \alpha, \beta, \theta) \propto \Pi_{t=1}^t \Pi_{k \in K_t} \Pi_{j \in J_k} \Phi(\alpha_k + \beta_k \theta_{t,j})^{v_{t,k,j}}$$
$$(1 - \Phi(\alpha_k + \beta_k \theta_{t,j}))^{1 - v_{t,k,j}}$$

is the sampling density. The identification problems that plague these models are resolved through the use of semi-informative prior distributions. The model is estimated using Markov chain Monte Carlo (MCMC) methods.

The first set of results is produced using a constant ideal point model. The authors note that the results display a good deal of face validity: Justices Marshall, Warren, Brennan, and Fortas are on the left, and Harlan, Burger, Rehnquist, and Scalia are on the right. The posterior standard deviations are generally small with the ideal points of moderates being estimated with more precision than those of extremists. Finally, the results correlate well with existing measures of judicial preferences. This preliminary analysis demonstrates that the model produces sensible estimates.

The results of the dynamic ideal point model demonstrate that many justices trend. Black, Frankfurter, and Thomas trend conservative, whereas Marshall, Brennan, Blackmun, Stevens, and Souter trend toward liberalism. Warren, Clark, and Powell do not trend. Martin and Quinn demonstrate that the results do not depend on the choice of prior distributions. Using the Bayesian method, it is also possible to compute the posterior probability that a given justice's ideal point in one term is greater than that justice's ideal point in another term, the location of the median justice, and the location of the median on the estimated judicial dimension. The conclusion to be drawn from these results is that the preferences of some (but not all) justices change over time, and this change is often monotonic. A constant measure of judicial preferences is not appropriate for explaining longitudinal judicial decision making over time.

The empirical model in this paper is not deductively derived from a theoretical model; in effect, the two models are one and the same. The point of using the empirical model, however, is not to test the theoretical model. No truth claims are made about either model. In fact, the claims made about the empirical model are more along the lines that the results are "sensible" and that the resulting measures should be regarded as meaningful. The results answer an important question (do judicial preferences change over time?) while at the same time providing a useful measurement tool for further investigation. Measurement is fundamental to all conceptions of science, and no one would argue with the scientific status of the Martin and Quinn paper.

Measurement is also the purpose of our next example. Treier and Jackman (2008) seek to improve upon existing country-level measures of democracy. These measures are often used as independent variables in research studying the "democratic peace" and the link between democracy and economic development. One common measure, known as a Polity score, is produced by weighting various indicators from the Polity IV data set. These indicators, based on the coding of experts, include the competitiveness of executive recruitment and the regulation of participation. The scores are created by combining these (mostly ordinal) indicators using a weighting scheme determined in advance. Treier and Jackman (2008) identify two problems with the aggregate measure. First, the aggregation scheme or scoring rule is quite simple and generally has the effect that a one-unit change in one indicator has the same effect as a one-unit change in another indicator. Second, the scores are often used in regression analyses without accounting for measurement error, and the simple aggregation scheme does not allow the analyst to estimate the measurement error.

Treier and Jackman's (2008) solution to these problems is to treat democracy as a latent variable and estimate democracy scores using a Bayesian ordinal item-response statistical model. The approach is similar to factor analysis, but is more flexible and permits the analyst to estimate the latent variable—democracy, in this case—and account for measurement error around that estimate. The weights placed on each component of the measure are also determined as part of the estimation, rather than being fixed in advance. Treier and Jackman describe the setup of the model as follows:

Let $i = 1, \ldots, n$ index country-years and $j = 1, \ldots, m$ index the Polity indicators. Let $k = 1, \ldots, K_j$ index the (ordered) response categories for item j. Then our model is

$$Pr(y_{ij} = 1) = F(\tau_{j1} - \mu_{ij})$$

$$\vdots \quad \vdots$$

$$Pr(y_{ij} = k) = F(\tau_{jk} - \mu_{ij}) - F(\tau_{j,k-1} - \mu_{ij})$$

$$\vdots \quad \vdots$$

$$Pr(y_{ij} = K_j) = 1 - F(\tau_{j,K-1} - \mu_{ij})$$

where $\mu_{ij} = x_i\beta_j$, x_i is the latent level of democracy in country-year i, y_{ij} is the i-th country-year's score on indicator j, and $F(\cdot)$ is a function mapping from the real line to the unit probability interval, defined here as the logistic CDF $F(z) = 1/(1 + exp(-z))$. The slope parameter β_j is the *item discrimination parameter*, tapping the extent to which variation in the scores on the latent concepts generates different response probabilities. ... τ_j is a vector of unobserved thresholds for item j, of length K_{j-1}, that follow an ordering constraint implied by the ordering of the responses, i.e., $\tau_{ja} < \tau_{jb}$, $\forall\, a < b$, $\forall\, j$.

(Treier and Jackman 2008, 205)

The model is estimated via MCMC methods after appropriate identification restrictions are imposed. There are several findings that emerge from the analysis. First, there is substantial divergence between the Polity scores and the item response theory measures for high and low levels of the Polity scores. Second, measurement error looms large in the model. For instance, once measurement error is accounted for, it is difficult to distinguish the United States from more than 150 other countries in terms of their level of democracy. Third, some of the Polity indicators tap latent democracy better than others, which implies that the existing Polity scores are not using the information contained in the indicators in an optimal way.

As in our other examples, Treier and Jackman are clear about the intended purpose of their empirical model: constructing a better measure of democracy. The model aids in the construction of this measure, and they argue that their approach is superior to the ad hoc approach used in earlier efforts. As in our other examples, no theory is tested and no claims of truth abound.

The final broad use of empirical models is characterization, which we previously described as a method of determining the facts, settling policy questions, or spotting provocative associations. Consider a study by Herron and Wand (2007) on assessing partisan bias in voting technology. The study concerns questions regarding the use of Accuvote voting machines during the 2004 presidential race in

New Hampshire. After the election, there were allegations that precincts that used the Accuvote system reported low vote totals for John Kerry. A quick study just after the election prompted a recount paid for by Ralph Nader.

The analysis begins by considering voting patterns grouped by type of voter technology. The data are New Hampshire presidential and gubernatorial vote shares over 234 towns in the 2000, 2002, and 2004 general elections. An overdispersed binomial model shows a mild significant difference between towns using Accuvote machines and towns using a different technology (Optech). A significant difference between the distribution of 2004 Kerry shares in Accuvote towns and the distribution of shares in Optech towns was also found using a bootstrapped Kolmogorov-Smirnov test. A differences-in-differences analysis of presidential and gubernatorial elections found similar results. These results indicate that there were problems in 2004 and also in 2000 and 2002. The authors, however, caution against a causal interpretation because the voting technologies were not randomly distributed across the precincts.

Determining whether the voting technology was causal requires an analysis that does not confound pre-election differences between precincts and differences in the means by which the precincts counted the votes. To that end, Herron and Wand provide two sets of analyses. The first is a series of precinct-level regressions. Weighted least squares regressions and overdispersed grouped logistical regressions are run. The latter models are analyzed with an estimator that is robust to outliers, which is important because both left-hand-side and right-hand-side variables may have been produced by an irregular process (biased voting technology). The results provide no support for allegations of partisan bias.

The second set of analyses uses multivariate propensity score matching to avoid making the kinds of strong assumptions that are unavoidable when using parametric models. The matching analysis also helps ensure that cases being compared have common support on the right-hand-side variables. The matching analysis consists of three separate analyses, where each analysis considers two of the three voting technologies available in New Hampshire. The results from the matching analysis closely reflect those of the regression analysis. No evidence was found for the claim that Accuvote machines undercounted the Kerry vote.

As in the previous examples, the empirical models used in the Herron and Wand study are not explicitly derived from theory. No deductively derived hypotheses are tested. No inferences are made to observations not in the study, and there is no need for the data to be a random sample. The goal is to answer a policy question (is the technology biased?), and no claims regarding the truth of the models in question are necessary. The arguments made by Herron and Wand instead regard the useful characteristics of their models in answering the basic question.

We should also note at this point that these three categories—prediction, measurement, and characterization—are not mutually exclusive. The Martin and Quinn study, much like the Herron and Wand work, answers an important substantive question and thus may be regarded as characterization; the model might also be used to predict future decisions of the justices. We might also profitably regard the Poole and Rosenthal paper as an example of an empirical model that is useful for the measurement of congressional ideal points. Similarly, the Herron and Wand paper could be seen as a measurement example. That these categories are fluid in no way diminishes the point that these papers are exemplars of science and yet sport none of the features political scientists have come to regard as scientific. Our next example typifies models with multiple purposes.

Diermeier, Keane, and Merlo (2005) (DKM) study the factors that influence the career decisions of members of Congress. To describe this choice process, DKM construct a structural model in which members of Congress are assumed to solve a dynamic optimization problem regarding their career decisions.[20] Specifically, every two years, a House member makes the following choice: run for reelection, run for a higher office, or leave Congress.[21] The value of running for reelection is modeled as the expected value of remaining in office plus the expected value of losing the seat and making an alternate career decision. The values for the other choices are modeled similarly. The member of Congress picks the alternative that maximizes the present value of benefits. By modeling individuals who choose to remain in Congress as well as those who choose to retire, DKM avoid the selection problems that typically plague analyses of this kind. The dynamic optimization problem for a House member is constructed with thirteen equations, including the probabilities of reelection, the expected value of each choice, and the specification of state variables affecting the prospects for reelection.

Numerous variables linked to career decisions are fed into this optimization model, including biographical data, committee membership, scandals, wages, important legislative accomplishments, and postcongressional data. DKM clearly have two purposes in mind for this model: characterization and prediction. They characterize the data by using the empirical model to estimate several features of congressional careers. For example, the authors determine which factors have the greatest influence on several values: the probability of reelection, the probability of election to the Senate, the likelihood of appointment to a prestigious committee, and the likelihood of legislative achievements. (These values enter into calculations of the expected value of remaining in office and the expected value of retirement.) DKM also describe the rewards to serving in Congress, finding that the nonpecuniary rewards far outweigh the monetary rewards, with a major legislative accomplishment conferring about $350,000 of nonpecuniary benefits on a House member. (During the time period covered by the study, salaries for members of Congress averaged about $120,000 in 1995 dollars.) The authors also estimate which factors most directly influence postcongressional wages, finding that the marginal returns from seniority decline rapidly. Finally, the authors are able to estimate the value of a seat in Congress, estimating the value of a House seat in 1995 dollars to be about $600,000, with a Senate seat worth about $1.6 million. One of the benefits of the structural model is that it organizes a massive data set, enabling researchers to create a more complete picture of the career decisions made by members of Congress.

DKM also use the model for prediction by conducting a series of policy "experiments" concerning the likely effects of two policy changes: term limits and increases in congressional wages. The predictions are generated easily by simply making changes to the monetary compensation of members (in the case of increased wages), or by forcing a candidate to leave office after a certain number of terms (in the case of term limits). The model predicts that an increase in congressional wages is unlikely to change the behavior of members, whereas term limits would lead to reductions in the proportion of legislators who run for reelection. As the authors acknowledge, they are not able to assess how the pool of candidates for office would be affected by either change. For this reason, the policy "experiment" they conduct is a first step toward understanding the consequences of increasing wages or imposing term limits.

Nowhere in the article do DKM claim to be testing a theoretical model. They acknowledge from the outset that members of Congress have multiple goals, and that a focus on the reelection motivation does not get us far in assessing the value of congressional careers. They articulate clearly that they have two purposes, characterization and prediction, and they acknowledge the limitations of the empirical model that they estimate.

5.6 CONCLUSION

We devoted this chapter to empirical models. Our argument is that empirical models share many of the same characteristics as theoretical models—indeed, characteristics shared by all models. That is, empirical models are neither true nor false, have limited accuracy, are partial, and are purpose-relative. The main difference between theoretical models and empirical models is that empirical models are closer to the actual world than theoretical models. This closeness is necessary because empirical models only produce useful results when united with data and the current state of statistical science. Unlike theoretical models, empirical models without these additional elements are of little use.

The second major part of our argument focuses on the uses of empirical models. We argued that empirical models are useful devices for prediction, measurement, and characterizing a data set. We provided examples of each of these uses that any political scientist would regard as scientific. At the same time, we disputed that empirical models are any good at the one thing that many political scientists assume they are good at—theory testing. The culprit, as it has been throughout this book, is H-D. We demonstrated that empirical models cannot be used to test theoretical models through the use of deductively derived hypotheses. The failure occurs regardless of the inferential approach taken. In the next chapter, we offer a way that theoretical models and empirical models can work together fruitfully.

Explanation

To explain the phenomena in the world of our experience, to answer the question "why?" rather than only the question "what?", is one of the foremost objectives of all rational inquiry; and especially, scientific research in its various branches strives to go beyond a mere description of its subject matter by providing an explanation of the phenomena it investigates.

—Philosophers CARL HEMPEL AND PAUL OPPENHEIM

6.1 INTRODUCTION

In the previous two chapters, we detailed the various uses for theoretical models and empirical models. Here we consider how theoretical models and empirical models interact. The question is not as easy as some in the profession would have us believe. One of the themes of this book is that theoretical models are never confronted with data. Instead, theoretical models are confronted with models of data, or empirical models, and these two types of models represent different things. A theoretical model represents a real-world system, whereas an empirical model represents the relationships and dependencies in a data set. Unfortunately, the real-world system and the data set are only loosely aligned even under the best of circumstances. Given that there is no testing relationship or even a strictly logical relationship between these kinds of models, the interaction between them is not obvious. In general, we do not believe that theoretical and empirical models need to be combined to achieve scientific advancement; in

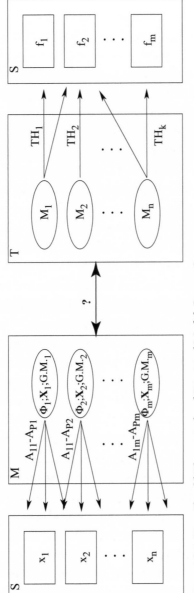

Figure 6.1 How Should Theoretical and Empirical Models Interact?

earlier chapters, we provided examples of research in which theoretical models and empirical models make stand-alone contributions to the discipline. That being said, there are legitimate reasons for pairing the two kinds of models, and we discuss those in this chapter.

This chapter's question is depicted in figure 6.1. On the right-hand side is a theory T comprising n theoretical models, each of which represents some features f_j of a real-world system S. On the left-hand side is a model space M comprising m empirical models, each of which models the relationships that exist in the real-world data S. What is the relationship, if any, that exists between theoretical and empirical models?

Stigum (2003) poses a similar question regarding what he calls the theory-data confrontation. Two worlds exist in Stigum's view: a theory universe and a data universe, which are not directly commensurable with one another. The theory universe comprises theoretical objects that describe "toys in a toy economy" (3). The variables in the data universe "live and function in a socially constructed world of ideas" that has little to do with true social reality (4). The riddle, then, is how to combine "elements from a toy economy with elements from a socially constructed world of ideas" to learn something of social reality (4).

Stigum's answer to his riddle is bridge principles "that stipulate the mapping between theoretical variables ... and their statistical counterparts" (Hoover 2006). These bridge principles can be quite complex, and indeed, some are models in and of themselves. Measurement models of theoretical concepts are an example. Bridge principles are, in many ways, reminiscent of correspondence rules in the Received View. Stigum, however, claims that the two are different in that bridge principles reflect the views of the individual researcher and are not part of the theory universe as correspondence rules would be.

Our argument is quite different and arises through a consideration of maps. The question is why you would ever use two different maps at perhaps different levels of abstraction. The first thing to note is that maps are not used to test one another. The "tests" a map undergoes are tests of its usefulness for achieving a particular purpose, not tests to determine whether another map is "correct" in some ill-defined sense. An individual using a subway map to navigate the subway constitutes a test of the map. There are, however, very practical reasons why someone might use two maps. Consider the Boston highway map in figure 3.2. First, we might consult this map or one like it to help construct the walking map of Boston in figure 3.3. The map in figure 3.2 could, for example, help identify and define the boundaries of the new map. Similarly, the map in figure 3.2 could help identify the macro-structures, such as highways, that need to be included in the new map to help with orientation.[1] Second, someone driving from the city of Revere to the city of Quincy along Route 1A might want to clarify precisely how Route 1A connects with Route 1 in downtown Boston or discover whether Route 3A connects with Route 93. A driver looking for a particular address may also want to consult a more precise map that details the many one-way streets in downtown Boston. Finally, one map may help explain features of another map. A driver may wonder why Route 1 becomes so curvy north of the city of Chelsea. A glance at a U.S. Geological Survey map would reveal the natural contours of the landscape that the road had to follow.

Our claim in this chapter is that theoretical models and empirical models interact in the same ways that different maps do. That is, a theoretical model can often be used to help identify an empirical model. Empirical models, on the other hand, can often be used to clarify the details of a theoretical model. We touched on these points briefly in chapters 4 and 5 when we noted that the generation of robust empirical generalizations can be spurs to theory development and that theory is sometimes necessary for identification. Our focus here is on the third way that models can interact—namely, that one can explain the other. Theoretical models can be used to explain findings or generalizations produced by empirical models. Empirical models, on the other hand, cannot provide explanations. The need to explain empirical findings provides a strong justification for combining theoretical and empirical models.

Before addressing the interactions between models, we discuss existing justifications for the insistence that the gap between theory and empirical analysis "seriously impairs scientific progress" (*Overview* 2008) and that "the scientific study of politics requires the empirical testing of theoretical models" (Aldrich and Alt 2003, 310). These justifications, to the extent that they exist, are focused solely on the issue of model testing.

6.2 EXISTING JUSTIFICATIONS FOR LINKING THEORETICAL AND EMPIRICAL MODELS

Explicit calls for linking theoretical and empirical models in political science go back at least as far as Aldrich (1980) and Achen (1983) and include, among others, Bartels and Brady (1993), Morton (1999), Achen (2002), Aldrich and Alt (2003), Granato and Scioli (2004), Aldrich, Alt, and Lupia (2007), and Granato, Lo, and Wong (2010).[2] Nearly all of these justifications are framed in terms of improved theory testing, the least persuasive use of empirical models. Aldrich, Alt, and Lupia (2007), for example, note that the participants in a workshop convened by the Political Science Program of the National Science Foundation were tasked "to find ways to improve the value and relevance of theoretical work by crafting it in ways that made key aspects of new models more amenable to empirical evaluation." Granato and Scioli (2004, 313) write that if the discipline continues its current practices, "we will find ourselves with a limited foundational basis for evaluating our models, unsure of their strength and too often unable to know where they went wrong." Similarly, Morton (1999, 24) writes "I aim to explore, in a straightforward manner, how empirical analysis has, can, and should be used to empirically evaluate formal models in political science." Granato, Lo, and Wong (2010, 784) see an "overall inattention in relating theoretical specifications to applied statistical tests," and argue that linkages between theoretical models and empirical models provide "the necessary transparency between theory and test to aid in valid hypothesis testing." Even Achen (2002, 441), who provides the most sophisticated justification—one cited at length in Aldrich, Alt, and Lupia (2007)—notes that his discussion emphasizes "methodology as the testing of theory."

Putting aside the issue of whether empirical models are good at testing theoretical models, these justifications are vague regarding their very premises: how previous practices harm the discipline, and how better theory testing improves the discipline. There is no evidence that continuing our current practices might "delay, or worse, derail the momentum generated over the past 40 years" (Granato and Scioli 2004, 313). Aldrich, Alt, and Lupia (2007) cite as evidence of "excessive specialization" the case of a *single* formal paper (by Austen-Smith), although they "believe there are many," with a low number of citations and no empirical evaluations (at the time of their writing). The authors speculate, "One would think that Austen-Smith's model could inform and advance empirical work," noting that the "narrative is clearly argued and the logic expertly presented." They argue that at a minimum, Austen-Smith's model suggests a variety of ways of evaluating causal claims made in the empirical literature. The clear implication is that Aldrich, Alt, and Lupia believe that without pairing the model with an empirical evaluation, Austen-Smith's modeling effort is wasted.

Achen (2002, 442) provides the strongest argument for combining theoretical and empirical models. His concern is the proliferation of estimators available to political scientists. He argues that microfoundations for statistical specifications are necessary to reduce specification uncertainty and provide intellectual coherence in empirical models. There are problems with this view, however. First, Achen provides no argument specifying how the use of more theoretically justified empirical models moves the field forward toward some goal. The absence of such an argument is a common theme among those advocating for better (in the sense of more theoretically justified) testing. Second, Achen (2002, 440) argues that estimators with microfoundations can be checked for errors against other estimators: "When logit follows from a formal model and power logit does not, but power logit fits better, then we know something is wrong in the formal theory supporting logit or in the implementation of the logit specification."

The disjunction in the latter part of the quote is not an accident. We cannot know that something is wrong in the formal theory supporting the logit because the fault may lie in the implementation (i.e., the rest of the model specification beyond the functional form) of the logit. Here, in the literature, is an acknowledgment of the Quine-Duhem problem that we discussed in chapter 2.[3] Even if we held the rest of the specification constant, it is unclear what is to gained from the test. Different functional forms may well imply different arrangements of variables (compare, for example, Signorino 1999 and Bueno de Mesquita and Lalman 1992).

We should add that interpreting Achen (2002) as primarily being about testing is to misread the piece. While claiming that testing is important, Achen (2002, 442) argues that "the discovery of thoroughly reliable quantitative generalizations with theoretical bite is often more crucial to the discipline than theory testing," noting that "a theory needs things to explain." We discussed the use of empirical models to produce generalizations in chapter 5, and we pick up the theme of explanation in the next section.

6.3 EXPLANATION

In political science, a model is a means to an end, rather than an end in and of itself. These ends, as we have already demonstrated, are quite varied and include organizing a seemingly disparate set of empirical observations, describing the statistical dependencies within a data set, and prediction. For this reason, we have argued that a model must be evaluated with respect to its particular purpose.

Despite the many uses to which models can be put, there exists a single overarching goal that serves to unite the disparate purposes of social scientific models: explanation.[4] Elster (2007, 9), for example, argues that explanation is the most important job of the social sciences, "to which others are subordinated or on which they depend." King, Keohane, and Verba (1994, 53) argue for a methodology that features explanation as the ultimate goal. Moreover, research projects should not be undertaken, they argue, unless those projects represent a step toward an explanation for a phenomenon (15). Tetlock and Belkin (1996b, 17) claim that the "ultimate social science goals" are "logically consistent, reasonably comprehensive and parsimonious, and rigorously testable explanations," and in a widely used text on methodology in political science, Van Evera (1997, 17) constructs a list of attributes for judging a theory's quality, with "large explanatory power" topping the list.

Explanation is equally important to purely qualitative researchers. Mahoney and Goertz (2006, 230), for example, argue that "a core goal of qualitative research is the explanation of outcomes in individual cases," with the main purpose being to "identify the causes of these specific outcomes for each and every case that falls within the scope of the theory under investigation." Gerring's (2007) work on case study research contrasts how the methodology of a case study changes depending on whether the author wishes to generalize across several cases (a "generalizing case study") or is interested in studying a single outcome. In both situations, though, Gerring refers to the research as providing explanations, albeit with varying degrees of generality (208). Similarly, case studies focusing on multiple cases (the "cross-case" study) share a common element with case studies focused on within-case variation: "the explanation of a population of cases" (21).

6.3.1 What Constitutes an Explanation?

Having argued that explanation is the crucial goal of political science, it is incumbent upon us to provide a discussion of what it means to explain. The debate over what constitutes an explanation, particularly a scientific explanation, has been a staple of the philosophical literature since publication of Hempel and Oppenheim's (1948) classic article, "Studies in the Logic of Explanation," and we have no intention of wading into the details of all the various battles. Instead, we summarize the two main currents of thought regarding the nature of explanation and demonstrate that political scientists have made use of both traditions. What these explanation accounts have in common is that the identification of a cause is an insufficient basis for making a claim to explanation. For this reason, we argue theoretical models are far more likely to contain explanations than empirical models.

The two main currents of thought regarding the nature of explanation—Salmon (1992, 33) refers to them as "grand traditions"—are the unification approach and the causal-mechanical approach. The former has its roots in logical positivism and considers an explanation to be a model or an argument that unites a large number of empirical regularities using only a small number of assumptions. The second tradition sees explanation as rooted in the causal mechanisms that lead to outcomes. We begin with unification and the now familiar strains of logical positivism (see chapters 2 and 3). The difficulties the logical positivists encountered with providing a theory of explanation help us understand later developments.

LOGICAL POSITIVISM AND UNIFICATION

By the tenets of logical positivism, to explain is to show that the phenomenon in question was to be expected (Hausman 1992). That is, an explanation consists of a set of conditions, which if true, is sufficient to produce the phenomenon. Another way to look at it is that explanation takes the form of a logical argument. In chapter 2, we detailed the parts of such an argument: general laws, initial conditions, and the event to explained. Under this model, known as the deductive-nomological (D-N) model (or more generally as the covering law model), if the event to be explained can be deduced from the general laws and initial conditions, then the argument can be called an explanation.

Hempel and Oppenheim (1948) present the classic example. When a mercury thermometer is dunked in hot water, there is a temporary drop in the mercury column, which is followed by a rapid rise. The explanation is that the hot water first expands the glass tube, which is why the mercury initially drops. When the heat reaches the mercury, it expands at a faster rate than the glass tube, causing the mercury to rise. The general laws are the laws of the thermic expansion of mercury and glass. The initial conditions are a glass tube partially filled with mercury that is then immersed in hot water. From these antecedents, we can deduce the behavior of the thermometer.

As a companion to the D-N account, Hempel (1962) put forward a probabilistic version called the inductive-statistical or I-S account, where the general laws in the former are replaced by statistical laws in the latter. With a statistical law among the explanans, it is no longer possible to derive the explanandum deductively. It is possible, Hempel argues, to state that the explanandum should hold with high probability. Hempel's example is a statistical law of the sort that the probability of reducing the symptoms of hay fever is high when a certain allergy medication is taken. An allergy sufferer who takes the medication is likely to see his or her symptoms subside.

Problems with the D-N account arose shortly after its introduction. One problem concerned what van Fraassen (1980) called the "asymmetries of explanation." In these kinds of examples, two arguments, both of which meet the D-N criteria for an explanation, are the inverses of one another. The asymmetry refers to our intuition that one argument seems explanatory and the other does not. The flagpole example is well known. We can deduce the length of a flagpole's shadow from the height of the flagpole, the position of the sun, and the application of trigonometry. However, we can also deduce the height of the flagpole from the length of the shadow and the angle of elevation. We readily accept the former argument (height → length) as an explanation, but not the latter (length → height).

A second problem concerns examples that contain causal irrelevancies, although the D-N account accords them the status of explanations. The best known example comes from Salmon (1971). The argument is that men who regularly take birth control pills do not get pregnant; George took birth control pills regularly; George avoided getting pregnant. This argument is a perfectly sound explanation according to the D-N account, but the act of taking birth control pills is, of course, irrelevant to the fact that George did not get pregnant. The D-N account offers no way of distinguishing between relevant arguments and irrelevant arguments.

Hempel's I-S account also ran into troubling counterexamples. The most famous of these is the case of general paresis, a paralysis disorder affecting the brain and central nervous system caused by untreated syphilis (Scriven 1959). General paresis is a counterexample to the I-S account because untreated syphilis is the only way to contract the disease, but the probability of contracting general paresis from untreated syphilis is quite low. Thus, although we would accord untreated syphilis status as an explanation for general paresis, it does not meet the high probability threshold required by Hempel.

The postwar literature on scientific explanation can be seen as a series of successive attempts to deal with the counterexamples just described. The natural successor to the D-N account within the same tradition is the unification conception first developed formally by Friedman (1974) and corrected and extended by Kitcher (1981, 1989). Kitcher even describes unification as being the "unofficial theory" behind the covering law model. Although the details of the unificationist account have become quite complex, the basic idea is simple: scientific explanation consists of unifying a number of empirical regularities with a minimum number of theoretical concepts or assumptions. Central to the account is the idea of an argument pattern. Kitcher (1981, 514) contends that the explanatory power of Newton's *Principia* lies in its "demonstration that one *pattern* of argument could be used again and again in the derivation of a wide range of accepted sentences." By the same token, Darwin in *Origin of the Species* demonstrates how his pattern can be applied to a large number of biological phenomena.

CAUSAL-MECHANICAL

The causal-mechanical account of explanation has its roots in the problems of the logical positivist account and in attempts to portray explanation solely in statistical terms. Salmon (1971) argued that the logical positivists had lost sight of the idea of a cause, and this gap led him to posit the statistical-relevance (S-R) account. The intuition behind the account is that explanations must cite causes, and causal relationships are captured by statistical relevance relations. Thus, an event or attribute C is statistically relevant to another event or attribute E given some population or background B, if and only if

$$Pr(E|B.C) \neq Pr(E|B).$$

That is, an event or attribute C is a cause of another event or attribute E if and only if the conditional probability of E given B (the population or background) and C is different from the conditional probability of E given B. Thus, for C to be a cause of an event E, C must be statistically relevant to E. Explaining an event by this account requires four steps (Dowe 2000, 167). The first step is to define the prior probability of E relative to a reference class or background. Second, the reference class is divided into relevant partitions. (A relevant partition comprises cells where the probability of E is different.) Third, the posterior probabilities for each cell are required. Fourth and finally, an individual is located in one of the cells. Salmon's example concerns an American teenager convicted of stealing a car. The reference class of American teenagers is divided into male and female and urban and rural. Selection of the relevant cell provides the explanation.

Salmon claimed that the S-R model could deal with examples that posed problems for the D-N account, such as causal irrelevancies. The birth control pills that George took are statistically irrelevant to his not becoming pregnant, so the taking of birth control pills could not be a cause of George's infertility. In addition, the S-R account differs from Hempel's I-S account because the explanandum need not follow from the explanans with high probability; it is enough that $Pr(E|B.C)$ differs from $Pr(E|B)$ even if both probabilities are low. Thus, the general paresis example is not a problem for Salmon's account.

Salmon (1984) himself gave up on the S-R model, arguing that statistical concepts alone are insufficient to account for explanation and that the "cause" needed to be put back in "because." He then embarked on a project to understand explanation as a physical process characterized by interactions between links in a causal chain. Salmon (1998, 71) explains his causal-mechanical account in this way:

> The basic idea—stated roughly and briefly—is that an intersection of two processes is a *causal interaction* if both processes are modified in the intersection in ways that persist beyond the point

of intersection, even in the absence of further interactions. When two billiard balls collide, for instance, the state of motion of each is modified, and those modifications persist beyond the point of collision. A *process* is *causal* if it is capable of transmitting a mark—that is, if it is capable of entering into a causal interaction.

An explanation, therefore, is "an effort to lay bare the mechanisms that underlie the phenomena we observe and wish to explain" (Salmon 1998, 71). That is, an explanation consists of showing the causal mechanisms and causal interactions that led to some event.

Although both the unification account and the causal-mechanical account have run into their own difficulties, they remain the two most widely accepted explications of what it means to explain.

6.3.2 Explanation in Political Science

What counts as an explanation in political science is murky. The dominant perspective holds that explanation comprises causation.[5] King, Keohane, and Verba (1994, 75) argue that to propose an explanation is to propose a cause: "Real explanation is always based on causal inference." For Van Evera (1997, 9), an explanation contains "the causal laws or hypotheses that connect the cause to the phenomenon being caused, showing how causation occurs." Gerring (2007, 5) notes that "within political science and sociology, the identification of a specific mechanism—a causal pathway—has come to be seen as integral to causal analysis, regardless of whether the model in question is formal or informal or whether the evidence is qualitative or quantitative." Elster (2007, 9) adopts an explicitly H-D framework where the explanandum must be an event, and "to explain it [the event] is to give an account of why it happened, by citing an *earlier event* as its cause." Green and Shapiro (1994, 191–92) indirectly address the issue by arguing that simplifying assumptions in a model are appropriate if they "distill into an explanation the factors that are causally responsible for outcomes."

Though there is agreement on causality as the basis for explanation, there is no agreement regarding what constitutes a cause. King, Keohane, and Verba (1994, 78), for example, write of causality strictly in counterfactual terms, and Elster (2007, 9) cites Hume and the idea of constant conjunction.[6] This lack of agreement over the definition of a cause leads to the murkiness regarding explanation. The end result is that social scientists make use of both traditions (unification and causal- mechanical) to provide explanations.

The unification conception of scientific explanation is not unknown, except perhaps in name, to the social sciences, and many explanations in political science and economics, particularly game theoretic ones, have this character to them. Elster (2007, 36–37), for example, defines "mechanisms" as "frequently occurring and easily recognizable causal patterns that are triggered under generally unknown conditions or with indeterminate consequences," and claims "that we can often explain behavior by showing it to be an instance of a general causal pattern, even if we cannot explain why that pattern occurred." In economics, Rappaport (1998, 195) refers to this kind of explanation as "explanation-what," which he defines in the following way:

> An explanation-what explains something as an *F*, with *F* representing general classificatory terms...Explanation by concept, however, is not merely classification. The events or phenomena explained must constitute a unified whole, with each individual phenomenon being part of the whole. Explanation-what is classification plus synthesis of phenomena into wholes.

An explanation-what explains by describing *what* something is, as opposed to *why* something is. Rappaport (1998, 201–203) uses the market for rental housing in Santa Monica, California, in April 1979 as an example. A citizen initiative froze the rents in Santa Monica for three months at their 1978 levels. Rappaport argues that economists explain what occurred in Santa Monica by the application of a model of a competitive market with price controls. The model both classifies the situation in Santa Monica and unifies the elements of the real market into a single explanation.

Similarly, Schelling (1978, 90), in a book on explanations of macrobehavior, writes of "families of models" in a way that is analogous to Kitcher's argument patterns: "Recognition of the wide applicability of a model, or of a family of models, helps in recognizing that one is dealing with a very general or basic phenomenon, not something specialized or idiosyncratic or unique."

Examples of models with wide applicability include critical mass, tipping, and lemons models, as well as the commons problem, the self-fulfilling prophecy model, the acceleration principle, and the ubiquitous Prisoner's Dilemma.

Explanations involving the Prisoner's Dilemma or the commons problem can be found through political science and political economy. Zupan (1991) is interested in understanding why many Americans choose to split their tickets, casting a ballot for one party when selecting who will represent them in Congress and a different party when selecting the president. Zupan notes that existing explanations of ticket splitting fail to account for a key fact: those who split their tickets typically pick Republicans for president and Democrats for Congress. Zupan proposes a Prisoner's Dilemma as an explanation for this phenomenon. He assumes that Democrats tend to "bring home the bacon" for their districts, and Republicans tend to advocate small government. A voter electing 1 of 435 members of Congress will have little effect on overall government spending levels, but the election of a Democrat can help ensure that pork is brought back to the district. This situation is a classic Prisoner's Dilemma. Even though voters prefer an outcome where no pork is procured to one where every district receives it, voters are always better off defecting to ensure that their district gets a piece of the pie. Given the Prisoner's Dilemma that operates in congressional voting, why do voters selecting Democrats for the House also vote for Republicans for president? A president is unlikely to help a specific district with projects, but he can help reduce the overall level of spending. Voters, therefore, get the best of both worlds: they are able to receive benefits for their districts while holding down spending overall. Presenting several sets of empirical patterns over time regarding split tickets and Democratic and Republican legislative and presidential behavior, Zupan (1991, 344) argues that "the Prisoner's Dilemma theory supplies at least a partial explanation for the schizophrenia displayed by voters."

Leventoğlu and Tarar (2005) are interested in explaining the use of public commitments by negotiators prior to the start of talks. As an example, they cite a Northern Ireland peace deal in the mid-1990s, where all of the parties involved made public commitments regarding their positions. Leventoğlu and Tarar argue that negotiators make such statements to gain bargaining leverage by increasing domestic audience costs. However, they explain the occurrence of suboptimal outcomes by demonstrating that a Prisoner's Dilemma arises when the negotiators face similar audience costs:

> If you believe that the other side is not going to make a public commitment, you want to make one in order to obtain the bargaining leverage of the one-sided case; and if you believe that the other side *is* going to make a public commitment, you also want to make one in order to mitigate the bargaining leverage that the other side will otherwise have over you. Thus, no matter what you believe that the other side is going to do, you are best off making a public commitment.
>
> (Leventoğlu and Tarar 2005, 423)

Thus, Leventoğlu and Tarar *explain* suboptimal bargaining outcomes by the application of a model, the Prisoner's Dilemma, that is well known to political scientists.

Like the Prisoner's Dilemma, the logic of the commons problem has been used to explain a wide variety of phenomena. The simple yet powerful explanation takes the following generic form. Consider a resource that has no clear ownership—a field used for grazing being the classic example used by Hardin (1968). Because no one entity owns the resource, a particularly pernicious collective action problem ensues. Although there may be some socially optimal rate at which the resource should be used—in the case of a field, perhaps only 100 cows should be permitted to graze the field per day—each individual user has no incentive to be concerned with the social optimum. Instead, a rational individual selects the usage that maximizes his utility, taking into account that others will behave in similar ways. The result is a socially suboptimal and potentially destructive use of the resource.

This logic has also been used by political scientists and economists to explain manifold fiscal issues, such as why legislators seek out large, inefficient projects for their districts when funding comes out of a broad tax base (e.g., Weingast, Shepsle, and Johnsen 1981) and why increasing the number of government entities with tax authority in a given geographic area leads to higher spending overall (Berry 2009). In both of these situations, government officials do not bear the full consequences of their decisions. Development economist William Easterly (2001), building on the work of Shleifer and Vishny (1993), argues that centralized corruption is less pernicious than decentralized corruption because a leader controlling bribe amounts has an incentive to not set bribes so high that businesses leave the country. Most notably, Elinor Ostrom (1990) has studied how institutions, both private and public, help address commons problems such as overfishing and water shortages. All of these solutions, however, hinge on an understanding of a situation as a commons problem.

The causal-mechanical tradition of explanation is also well known to the social sciences. Goldthorpe (2001, 8), for example, discusses causation as "generative process," by which he means a process "existing in time and space, even if not perhaps directly observable, that actually generates the causal effect of X on Y." Goldthorpe points to epidemiology, the hard science closest to the social sciences, and the debate over smoking and lung cancer as a case in point. Epidemiologists were able to establish a strong statistical association between smoking and lung cancer, but the establishment of an accepted causal connection had to wait for the delineation of a causal mechanism based on known carcinogens in cigarette smoke and other factors.

For political science examples, consider Pevehouse (2002), who examines the role of international organizations (IOs) in fostering democratization. Pevehouse does not have a formal model in his account, but he does have a verbal model, and he proposes three causal mechanisms linking the actions taken by regional IOs to regime change. First, IOs can generate diplomatic and economic pressures that in combination with internal forces can coerce autocratic regimes to liberalize. This mechanism begins with a schism in an authoritarian regime caused by an exogenous shock. The leaders of the regime may liberalize in an effort to beat back the threat to their legitimacy. External pressure from the IOs delegitimize the regime further, providing the impetus for democratization. Pevehouse argues that regional organizations are more effective at accomplishing this goal than individual states for two reasons. First, regional organizations lower transaction costs and provide a "highly visible forum to air complaints against member states" (523).[7] Second, regional organizations provide a unified front and therefore increase the legitimacy of the applied pressure.

The second mechanism Pevehouse proposes begins with elites, including business and military elites, who have strong incentives to fight liberalization, as they benefit from the status quo. Regional IOs weaken the opposition of these groups by lowering the risks faced by elites during democratization, which further weakens the autocratic leaders who rely on the elites to maintain power. This process occurs in two different ways. The first mechanism concerns credible guarantees for business elites. Membership in regional organizations may provide an external guarantee that property rights, among others, are to be protected, therefore lowering the costs of democratization and increasing the likelihood of its adoption. The second mechanism is a socialization process. Members of the military can be "socialized" to view their role as protecting the state from external (rather than internal) threats. This process occurs simply through interactions with military leaders from other states. Regional IOs can also provide guarantees by requiring a democratizing state to maintain resources for the military, as any alliance might, thereby alleviating fears of a move to democracy.

Although Pevehouse does not construct utility functions for the various actors in his model—authoritarian rulers, business leaders, members of the military—his approach nonetheless offers causal-mechanical explanations for how regional IOs can cause democratization among member states.[8]

Acemoglu and Robinson (2006), in their seminal work on the emergence of democratization and dictatorship, take a different approach from Pevehouse, focusing instead on the microfoundations of individual behavior. Out of several models in their book, we focus on a single model that demonstrates how the middle class plays a role in fostering democratic consolidation. The model features a society comprising the poor, the middle class, and the rich. In the model, the rich decide whether to mount a coup against the democratic leadership; they do so if the expected benefits outweigh the benefits of remaining in the democracy. The value of democracy versus a coup is determined by the extent of redistribution in the democracy. Policy in the democratic society is set by the median voter, who can propose a single tax rate applicable to all citizens. Revenues raised from these taxes are then redistributed to all citizens equally.

The causal mechanism works in the following way. Each voter wants to maximize his or her share of the pie. The poor always favor some redistribution because they always pay less in taxes than they receive in benefits for some positive tax rate. (The cost of raising revenue is what prevents the poor from setting a tax rate of 100 percent.) The rich never favor redistribution, since they always pay out more than they receive. The middle class favors positive redistribution if their income is low enough that they receive more in redistribution than they pay out in taxes (and in the associated losses that taxes produce). Therefore, if the median voter is poor or middle class when the middle class is relatively poor compared to the rich, then she prefers more redistribution and the higher tax rates necessary to fund it. This outcome, all else being equal, lowers the value of democratic consolidation for the rich, who pay for the redistribution, and thus increases the likelihood of a coup. The richer the median voter becomes, the less redistribution she favors, and the easier it is to set a tax rate that is low enough to prevent a coup and produce democratic consolidation. In other words, the selection of a tax rate and a redistribution policy by the middle class influences the incentives of the rich concerning coups versus democratic consolidation.

6.4 MODELS AS EXPLANATIONS

Our point in discussing the nature of explanation is not to choose between explanation as unification or explanation as causal mechanism. We have shown that political scientists make use of both types of explanation, and we see no reason why they should not continue to do so. Our goal is to analyze the conditions under which models can serve as explanations. Despite claims by political scientists to the contrary, the identification of a cause in and of itself is an insufficient basis for an explanation.

Before we can have this discussion, we must clarify the relationship between explanation and truth in order to dismiss the idea that truth is a necessary condition for an explanation. Van Fraassen (1980, 98) addresses the issue squarely: "to say that a theory explains some fact or other, is to assert a relationship between this theory and that fact, which is independent of the question whether the real world, as a whole, fits that theory." The arguments van Fraassen advances for this contention revolve around the unsavory conclusions that must follow from accepting the premise that explanations must be true. For instance, Newton's theory did not explain the tides because we now know that Newton's theory is not true. This must be the case despite the fact that we are quite normally willing to state that Newton's theory served as the explanation for the tides throughout the nineteenth century. In fact, if we accept the premise that explanations must be true, then Newton never explained anything. Furthermore, we must accept that we have no explanations at all because at any time we could observe phenomena that are inconsistent with our theories.

Van Fraassen also makes the argument that scientists themselves do not believe that explanations must be true. That a theory explains is for some scientists part of the evidence that leads to the theory's acceptance. Thus, the explanatory relation exists prior to any acceptance of the theory. Finally, social science practice itself reflects an understanding that explanations need not be true. Pitting "rival" or "competing" or "candidate" explanations against one another is a commonly employed technique throughout political science.

Having dispensed with the notion that explanations must be true, we turn to a discussion of what kinds of models can serve as explanations. That theoretical models often provide explanations is self-evident to a degree. As demonstrated in the previous section, theoretical models generally correspond to one or both accounts of explanation. Empirical models, however, seem to provide neither a sense of mechanism nor an argument pattern. We need to ask, then, whether empirical models can be explanations.

There is little argument in political science that statistical models cannot serve as explanations in and of themselves. This belief manifests itself in the relegation of statistical models to devices for *testing* explanations. As we have previously noted, the structure of most political science articles begins with a theoretical discussion that is sometimes formalized and sometimes not. The theoretical discussion is followed by hypotheses that the author derives from the theory, and the article ends with the introduction of a statistical model designed to test the derived hypotheses. The statistical model does not embody the theoretical model and instead comprises one or more variables associated with each of the hypotheses to be tested.

It is not just practice, however, that assigns statistical models to a nonexplanatory role. Many commentators on the social sciences agree. Little (1991, 178–79), for example, argues that there are no autonomous statistical explanations: "The statistical association does not establish the presence or character of a set of causal mechanisms connecting the variables. . . . The discovery of a statistical regularity among variables rather constitutes an empirical description of social phenomena that itself demands explanation."

Elster (2007, 8) largely agrees, arguing that "statistical explanations are incomplete by themselves, however, since they ultimately have to rely on intuitions about plausible causal *mechanisms*." Care must be taken in characterizing this agreement, however, because Little and Elster have different definitions of "mechanism." For Little (1991, 15), a causal mechanism "is a series of events governed by lawlike regularities that lead from the explanans to the explanandum." A causal mechanism, letting **C** be a condition and **E** an outcome, connects a series of C_i culminating in an **E** along with the laws that govern the transitions between the C_i.[9] For Elster (2007, 36), mechanisms are, as we noted earlier in the chapter, commonly occurring and recognizable causal patterns. Proverbs, according to Elster, are examples of what he means by causal mechanisms. A proverb "sums up, in one short phrase, a general principle, or common situation, and when you say it, everyone knows exactly what you mean" (Elster 2007, 37). Examples include "absence makes the heart grow fonder" and "opposites attract."

We agree with both Little and Elster, who embody the two forms of explanation already discussed. Elster's idea of causal mechanisms as frequently occurring causal patterns matches the unification account and Kitcher's argument patterns. Little's idea of a causal mechanism as a series of events is close to Salmon's causal-mechanical account of explanation. Empirical models, however, capture neither conception of a causal mechanism and therefore cannot provide explanations.

Admittedly, it is not immediately obvious that statistical models cannot capture either idea of a causal mechanism. A statistical model, at its most basic, is a description that helps a researcher understand what is happening in the data. The statistical model is thereby providing an argument, like the Prisoner's Dilemma, that applies to many (but not all) of the observations in the data set. In a very real sense, then, a statistical model does provide a recurring argument pattern. At the same time, some statistical models, such as structural models and dynamic models, seem to provide the sense of direction necessary for Little's conception of a causal mechanism.

The problem, however, is that it is nearly impossible to discern a single explanation from simply looking at an empirical model.

Consider a regression of the county-level vote for Woodrow Wilson in the 1916 election in New Jersey on three independent variables: the Wilson vote in 1912, a dummy variable for the beach counties (Monmouth, Ocean, Atlantic, and Cape May), and a dummy variable for counties (Bergen, Hudson, Essex, and Union) controlled by political machines (Achen and Bartels 2004). The variables "Beach County" and "Machine County" have negative effects on the 1916 Wilson vote, and Wilson's 1912 vote is positively correlated with Wilson's 1916 vote. Without additional context, it is impossible to know what to make of these relationships or what the authors were hoping to illustrate. Which variables are the "important" ones? Which variables are meant to act solely as controls? Is the explanation that party bosses can affect the vote? Or is it that beach counties are different from other New Jersey counties? Perhaps the point is that Wilson's 1916 vote can largely be explained by his 1912 vote. As it turns out, none of these guesses are correct. Achen and Bartels use the results of their regression to demonstrate that voters in New Jersey's beach counties punished the Wilson administration for shark attacks along the coast in the summer of 1916 although the administration was wholly blameless. There is no way to discern this intent from just looking at the model.

Perhaps it is easier to discern an explanation in an empirical model if a true cause can be discerned through experimental means. If to propose a cause is to propose an explanation (see King, Keohane, and Verba 1994), then the positive demonstration of a cause should be enough. However, even researchers who identify putative causes in their work acknowledge, sometimes tacitly, that their statistical models cannot provide explanations. These acknowledgments come in the form of suggested mechanisms to account for the observed causal association. Gerber and Green (2000) conduct a randomized field experiment involving nearly 30,000 registered voters in New Haven, Connecticut. The voters were divided randomly into treatment and control groups with the treatment groups receiving a nonpartisan get-out-the-vote message either by mail, telephone, or personal contact.[10] Gerber and Green find that personal canvassing increases voter turnout "substantially," while mail and telephone calls have either small or no effects.

Despite having identified what they believe to be a causal effect, Gerber and Green (2000, 662) feel that a gap remains:

> We know very little about the mechanism by which personal contact influences voting behavior or why impersonal forms of contact have less effect. Our experiments do not tell us whether personal contact enhances interest in politics, feelings of connectedness to the electoral system, the belief that elections are important, or a sense of obligation to participate.

Gerber and Green indicate that they plan to augment future field experiments with postelection surveys "to assess the psychological imprint left by canvassers" (662). What they are missing is a theoretical model to explain their finding. The results of such surveys will aid in the construction of such a model but will not provide an explanation on their own.

In situations where empirical findings exist, an explanation can be provided through the use of an organizational model. Shepsle and Weingast (1987), in a study of the foundations of committee power, construct an organizational model for the explicit purpose of providing an explanation. The authors note that congressional scholars had come to consensus around a number of stylized facts and anomalies, among which are committees as "gatekeepers" in their jurisdictions and that committees are deferred to by legislators. Among the anomalies are policy changes in a bicameral system caused by changes in the makeup of a single chamber and rarely employed procedures to diminish committees' gatekeeping power. About the stylized facts, Shepsle and Weingast (1987, 85) write,

> There is, however, a troublesome quality to this consensus. The items in this list (and there could undoubtedly be more) describe or label committee power, but they do not explain it. Explanations of these empirical regularities require a theory. In the case of each

of these stylized facts, that is, a theory is needed to determine why things are done this way.

The proposed explanation for committee power focuses on the rules in the legislature governing how bills are initiated, amended, and vetoed.[11] In their multidimensional spatial model, every congressional committee is assumed to have a specific policy jurisdiction over which it possesses monopoly proposal rights. If the committee declines to make a proposal, current policy remains in place. If the committee chooses to make a proposal, then other legislators can propose amendments to that legislation. Once the amending process is complete, the (potentially modified) legislation is voted on by the entire legislature. The committee has the right to exercise an ex post veto if it does not like the changed legislation.

Shepsle and Weingast argue that the committee's gatekeeping power at the proposal stage is somewhat limited in the absence of the ex post veto. Without this tool, bills may be amended by legislators in ways that make the committee worse off than if the policy remained unchanged. The committee does not initiate a bill when it believes this action might occur, even if there are potential policy proposals that would make both the committee and a majority of the legislature better off.[12] In other words, commitment problems prevent deals that could get done from actually getting done.

Once this veto is added, however, the committee knows that it can block any amended bill that makes it worse off than the status quo. The result is that the committee proposes a bill whenever there is a majority-preferred alternative to the status quo that also makes the committee better off. Such proposals are the only alternatives that can satisfy both the legislature as a whole and the committee. In this way, the addition of the ex post veto permits the committee to achieve policy outcomes better than the status quo more often.

Shepsle and Weingast claim that their model can explain many of the stylized facts that they list. For example, what many observers refer to as deference to the committee—for instance, making few amendments to a committee proposal—is explained by the ex post veto and the sequencing of decisions in the legislative process. These rules create an incentive structure and strategic environment that cause legislators to behave differently than they would in the absence of those rules. In other words, the rules can tell us *why* legislators would ever defer to a committee. A legislator who knows that the committee possesses this veto may not propose an amendment to a committee bill if she has reason to believe the committee would exercise its veto on the amended bill.

The ex post veto explains another form of apparent deference by legislators to the committee. Specifically, legislatures are often able to "discharge" a bill that a committee refuses to report out, often with a simple majority vote. Yet bills are rarely discharged, and deference is the typical explanation. For Shepsle and Weingast, the explanation comes from the rules. In many cases, a committee would use its ex post veto power to kill any bill the legislature discharged, making the act of discharge not worth the effort.

Two additional questions are raised by the argument that empirical models must rely on theoretical models for explanation. The first question is what if two theoretical models claim to explain the same set of empirical findings? In this case, we must fall back on the model evaluation criteria discussed in chapter 4. The second question is what if one theoretical model explains one set of empirical findings for a particular dependent variable, and another theoretical model explains a different set of empirical findings with the same dependent variable? In this case, we are sometimes faced with discriminating among rival explanations.

6.5 CHOOSING AMONG EXPLANATIONS

How to choose among explanations based on statistical evidence presents two challenges. The first problem is described in chapter 5: the deductive nature of hypothesis testing in political science and the deductive nature of statistical hypothesis testing prevent us from drawing direct conclusions about the explanation in question. The second problem is described in chapter 2: the fragile nature of statistical evidence makes the H-D method unsound. The first problem can be addressed by abandoning the goal of testing individual theoretical models and embracing the goal of comparative model testing (Clarke 2007a). The second problem cannot be solved, and so statistical evidence must always be viewed with a skeptical eye.

Comparative model testing can only tell us about the relative virtues of rival models. That is, we can make statements that model 1 is "better" in some sense than model 2, but both models could still be poor. Determining the one true explanation, to the extent that such a thing exists, is not an option. The assumption that the one true explanation is among the set of candidate explanations being compared is heroic. What is required in place of the search for the true explanation is the search for the best explanation. That is, given the set of explanations actually at hand, we want to pick the best performing explanation.[13]

6.5.1 Comparative Model Testing

Theoretical model testing in political science is defeated by the deductive nature of the procedure. Recall the verificationist logic from chapter 5, reproduced in figure 6.2 in its long form with D (the data follow a certain pattern) substituted for the "coefficient is correct."

Under verificationism, a theoretical model implies a research hypothesis, which in turn implies that the data follow a certain pattern.

$$(1) \ TM \ \rightarrow H_1$$

$$(2) \ \left. \begin{array}{l} H_1 \rightarrow D \\ D \end{array} \right\} \nvdash H_1$$

$$(3) \ \left. \begin{array}{l} TM \ \rightarrow H_1 \\ H_1 \end{array} \right\} \nvdash TM$$

Figure 6.2 Verificationism

Finding that the data do follow that pattern, however, does not confirm the research hypothesis because to do so would be to commit an affirming-the-consequent error. Similarly, finding that the research hypothesis holds does not confirm the theoretical model.

Resolving these problems requires replacing the conditional "if, then" statements ($\rightarrow$) in the logic with biconditional "if and only if" statements ($\leftrightarrow$). These changes are made in figure 6.3. The biconditional resolves the "affirming the consequent" problem in (2) and (3), and we can validly conclude that the theoretical model is supported.

In figure 6.3, (1) ends in H_1 and (2) begins with H_1 so we can reduce the logic of figure 6.3 to the logic in figure 6.4. If the theoretical model is a necessary and sufficient condition for the research hypothesis, and the research hypothesis is a necessary and sufficient condition for the data to follow an expected pattern, then the theoretical model is a necessary and sufficient condition for the data to follow an expected pattern. We can conclude that the theoretical model is supported because of the biconditional.

The logic in figure 6.4 raises the question of when or where in political science a statement could be made that the data follow an expected pattern if and only if the theory is true. Even in the physical sciences statements of this type are rare. We can, however, make statements using the biconditional when we compare a model with a direct rival.

$$(1) \ TM \leftrightarrow H_1$$

$$(2) \ \left.\begin{array}{c} H_1 \leftrightarrow D \\ D \end{array}\right\} \vdash H_1$$

$$(3) \ \left.\begin{array}{c} TM \leftrightarrow H_1 \\ H_1 \end{array}\right\} \vdash TM$$

Figure 6.3 Using the Biconditional

$$TM \leftrightarrow D \left.\vphantom{\begin{matrix}\\\\\end{matrix}}\right\} \vdash TM$$
$$D$$

Figure 6.4 The Reduced-Form Logic

Let TM_1 and TM_2 be rival theoretical models in figure 6.5, and let D be a data pattern consistent with there being no difference between the theoretical models (usually a test statistic equal to 0). If we find that the data do not conform to the expected pattern, $\neg D$, then we can validly conclude, because of the "if and only if" statement, that one theoretical model is better than the other.

The techniques used for comparing explanations empirically depend on whether the models to be compared are nested or non-nested. Two empirical models are nested when one of the models is a special case of the other. Two empirical models are non-nested when neither model is a special case of the other model (see Clarke 2001). When the two models are nested, standard tests familiar to most political scientists, such as the F test, can be used to discriminate between them. Non-nested testing is more difficult and requires the use of specialized tests such as the Cox test (Cox 1961); the J test (Davidson and MacKinnon 1981), which is a linearized version of the Cox test; the Vuong test (Vuong 1989); or the Clarke test (Clarke 2007b).

Consider Coate and Conlin (2004) on voter turnout, perhaps one of the most studied topics in political economy and political behavior. The authors propose a group rule–utilitarian model in which voters are divided into those who support a ballot referendum and those who do not. An individual voter decides whether to vote by constructing a rule that, *if followed by every citizen on his side*, maximizes that side's overall

$$TM_1 \equiv TM_2 \leftrightarrow D \left.\vphantom{\begin{matrix}\\\\\end{matrix}}\right\} \vdash TM_1 > TM_2$$
$$\neg D$$

Figure 6.5 Being Comparative

utility. The optimal voting rule takes the form of a threshold voting cost below which voters vote and above which they abstain. The voting rule depends on the values of five parameters: the proportion of eligible voters who support the proposal (characterized by two parameters of a Beta distribution); the individual cost of voting; the benefit to supporters of referendum approval; and the (negative) benefit to opponents of referendum approval. The model is estimated using data from small Texas elections regarding changes to local liquor laws.

Coate and Conlin want to compare their explanation of voter turnout with a version of the intensity model, under which voters receive greater payoffs from voting the more strongly they feel about the referendum under consideration. Under the intensity model, "voting is like cheering at a football game and you are more likely to cheer the more you care about the outcome" (Coate and Conlin 2004, 1494). The authors use a Vuong test (Vuong 1989) to compare the explanations, as the models are non-nested. The null hypothesis is that the two explanations are equally good; under the null, the Vuong test should take a value of 0. The results indicate that the group rule–utilitarian model outperforms the intensity model.

In a follow-up article, Coate, Conlin, and Moro (2008) estimate a pivotal voter model using the Texas liquor data and then use the Vuong test to compare the pivotal voter model with the intensity model. This time the intensity model outperforms the pivotal voter model. These two sets of results should not be interpreted as implying that either the intensity model or the pivotal voter model is useless. For example, all of the explanations may be simultaneously true. These tests were performed on small-scale elections data, and it may be that a pivotal voter model works best for some kinds of elections, and the intensity model works best for other kinds of elections. (We take up this issue in the next section.) It is more likely that none of these explanations are true, but the goal of comparative model testing is not to pick the true explanation but the best explanation. Finally, it is necessary to keep in mind that the results of such tests are completely dependent on the quality of the empirical models, the quality of the data, and the state of statistical science (the Quine-Duhem problem).

6.5.2 Is Choosing Necessary?

The desire to choose between explanations is concomitant with the desire to test theoretical models. Much of the time, however, choosing between explanations simply is not necessary. The reason is found in what van Fraassen (1980) refers to as the "pragmatics" of explanation. Consider the question: why did Germany invade Poland in 1939? What is really being asked here? There are four possibilities:

1. Why did *Germany* invade Poland in 1939?
2. Why did Germany invade *Poland* in 1939?
3. Why did Germany invade Poland *in 1939*?
4. Why did Germany *invade* Poland in 1939?

Question 1 asks why Germany, as opposed to some other state, such as Russia, invaded Poland in 1939. Question 2 asks why Germany invaded Poland, as opposed to another neighboring state. Question 3 asks why did the invasion occur specifically in 1939 and not in 1938 or 1940. The final question asks why Germany invaded Poland instead of exercising other options.

The point of rehearsing these questions is that each asks for a different explanation. The answer to Question 2 usually references the German desire to regain territory lost under the Treaty of Versailles. The answer to Question 3 usually concerns the time it took Germany to rearm and mobilize. There is no need to choose between these explanations, however, for each answers a different question.

Multiple explanations can also exist without any single explanation being false. Consider the 2009 crash of Colgan Air Flight 3407 outside of Buffalo, New York. Explanations for the crash include human error (the captain did not react properly to an imminent stall), lax regulation (the captain failed four Federal Aviation Administration check flights, both pilots were fatigued), the weather (the captain, fearing icing, may have overreacted after an icing video distributed by the airline), unrealistic training (the use of simulators that fail to mimic in-flight conditions), equipment (the airspeed indicator lacked low-speed awareness features), and inadequate airline standard operating procedures. Perrow (1999, 7) argues that in any complex system, such as an airplane, accidents are the result of the interaction of multiple failures. Essentially, all of these explanations are both simultaneously correct and simultaneously wrong. Choosing between them is unnecessary, as they all contributed to the crash. Of course, we should also note that which explanation appeals to a particular group depends on who belongs to the group. The pilots union blames the training, the regulators blame human error, and the airlines attempt to avoid legal liability.

The events that we study in political science are no less complex than an airplane crash and are most likely infinitely more complex. Elections and wars do not have single explanations, but a multitude of explanations that interact to produce the outcome. Thus, whether you take an institutional approach or a behavioral approach to explaining political phenomena, there is always some evidence that can be evinced in favor of your choice. Consider Allison's (1971) *Essence of Decision*, in which the author evaluates three explanations—he calls them models—of the events that took place during the Cuban missile crisis. The three explanations are the rational actor model, the organizational politics model, and the governmental politics model. Instead of arguing that one model or explanation is correct, Allison (1971, 251) argues that the three models produce different explanations of different events:

> Spectacles magnify one set of factors rather than another and thus not only lead analysts to produce different explanations of problems that appear, in their summary questions, to be the same, but also influence the character of the analyst's puzzle, the evidence he assumes to be relevant, the concepts he uses in examining the evidence, and what he takes to be an explanation.

He goes on to argue that the three explanations are not completely incompatible with one another and each has something to contribute to our understanding. He contends that combining the three explanations into a general explanation is unnecessary and possibly damaging:

> The developed sciences have little hesitation about partial models. The fact that additional factors are known to be relevant to a class of outcomes does not necessarily mean that it is always helpful to try to incorporate these factors into an analytic model. In contrast, the aspiring sciences tend to demand general theory. In satisfying this demand, they often force generalization at the expense of understanding. (275)

Choosing between explanations takes up an enormous amount of researchers' time and pages in journals. It is not always necessary, and both time and pages could be put to more productive use. There are no precise rules for determining whether to engage in explanation comparison, but we should always ask ourselves, "What exactly is to be gained from comparatively testing these explanations?" Instead of taking for granted that one explanation must always be the "winner," we should learn all that we can from the explanations we have.

6.6 CONCLUSION

Existing justifications for combining theoretical and empirical models fail to make the case that previous practices harmed the discipline and better theory testing improves the discipline. These rationales are based on assertion, anecdotes, and little evidence. In place of these weak justifications, we offer a reason for combining theoretical and empirical models that cannot be reduced to theory testing. Exactly as we might use one map to explain a second map, theoretical models can be used to explain the findings of empirical models, which are rarely explanations in and of themselves.

An explanation consists either of an argument that unites a large number of empirical regularities or the description of a causal chain leading to the occurrence of the phenomenon. Political scientists have made use of both traditions in their theoretical work. Empirical models are unable to capture convincingly either conception of a scientific explanation. The need to explain empirical findings therefore provides a strong justification for combining theoretical and empirical models.

Choosing between explanations on the basis of statistical evidence is difficult. It is possible, by embracing comparative model testing, to avoid the problems engendered by the deductive connections between models. The price we pay is that models can be compared only relative to one another. We may conclude that one explanation is better than another, but both explanations may be poor. Choosing between explanations, however, is not always necessary. What appear to be rival explanations may in actuality be explanations of different phenomena or partial explanations of complex events. Rival explanations that are incompatible with one another may all still provide important insights.

Conclusion

Models are to be used but not to be believed.

—Econometrician HENRI THEIL

7.1 INTRODUCTION

Political science as a discipline is heavily model-dependent, and the field is in need of a coherent framework for thinking about models and their uses. We provide just such a framework. The model-based view of science treats models as maps that are to be evaluated based on their usefulness for a specific purpose. This perspective is at odds with the field's move toward an insistence that theoretical models be tested by empirical models, and the associated conceit that work relying on combining theoretical and empirical models is superior to work relying on stand-alone models.

Underlying the drive toward combining theoretical and empirical work in the name of testing is an outdated and faulty understanding of science that has its roots in nineteenth-century physics. This view has not held any true currency for 40 years, but you would never know it from the attention lavished on it in fields such as political science that are overly concerned with being "scientific." The hypothetico-deductive (H-D) method has become the unchallenged "science" in "political science" without ever having undergone real scrutiny. We provide that scrutiny, and the method is found wanting.

7.2 REVIEW OF THE ARGUMENT

Our book begins by describing the "science" in political science. We demonstrate that there is a good deal of agreement among modern political scientists regarding what it means to be scientific. The method consists of writing down a theoretical model, deriving a hypothesis from the model, and testing the hypothesis. If the hypothesis holds in the world, then the theoretical model is confirmed. If the hypothesis does not hold in the world, then the theoretical model is disconfirmed. The method is known as H-D, and it suffuses the discipline. Our evidence includes direct quotes from top scholars, a well-known textbook, as well as a survey of peer-reviewed articles in top journals. H-D is even the logic underlying the statistical tests the field uses. The discipline's use of H-D is an outgrowth of the concern of pioneering political scientists with being scientific.

We make two central arguments in the rest of the book. First, testing theoretical models is not logically possible. This argument unfolds in chapter 2 (and again in chapter 5), where we discuss the problems with H-D. We make two main claims. One, deductions are truth-preserving; truth flows "down" a deductive model, not "up" it. Therefore, if the assumptions of a model are true, then the conclusion is true, and a test is not necessary. If the assumptions are not true, then the conclusion may be either true or untrue. Even if we were to test these conclusions, the test would not tell us anything about the theoretical model (truth does not flow "up" a deductive system). Thus, whether the assumptions of a theoretical model are true or not, a test of the conclusions derived from the model are uninformative. Two, H-D only works if the observation statements used to test the deduced hypotheses are secure. Theoretical models in political science, however, are not tested with data; they are tested with models of data, which are far from secure. The situation we face, then, is testing a model with another model, an issue we pick up again in chapter 6.

The second major argument of the book is that testing theoretical models is unnecessary and mistakes the true nature of models. This argument unfolds in chapter 3. Models are like maps. First, they are objects and thus neither true nor false. Talking about models in terms of truth and falsity is a category mistake. Models are also like maps in that they have limited accuracy, are partial, and most importantly, are purpose-relative (a point we address in depth in chapters 4 and 5). The model-based view of science systematizes these features. Following Giere (1990), a model is a system characterized by a definition. The relationship between the system defined in the model and a real-world system is asserted by theoretical hypotheses. A theoretical hypothesis asserts that an object—a system known as a model—is similar, in some respects and for some purpose, to another object, a real-world system. Similarity relations can be vague (less so if you point out the respects and degrees to which two objects are similar), but vagueness is preferable to precise but illusory standards. Theories under this view are simply collections of models.

In chapter 4, we provide a typology of theoretical models focusing on purpose, which provides a foundation for thinking about the usefulness of models in political science. Theoretical models serve in any one or more of four different roles: foundational, organizational, exploratory, and predictive. Foundational models are generally quite abstract and provide a basis for further model building or allow for adaptation to many different kinds of questions. Organizational models allow for a group of disparate empirical generalizations, theoretical results, or set of facts to be collected under a single framework. Exploratory models allow the investigation of causal mechanisms or motivations underlying phenomena of interest. True predictive theoretical models are rare in political science.

Empirical models are the concern of chapter 5. Empirical models cannot simply be theoretical models with an error term for two reasons. First, empirical models rely on information that can only come from the data. If these inputs are wrong, then the empirical model is wrong because it, too, has a deductive structure. Second, theory is general (even when about something specific), and data are specific, tied to particular places and times. Thus, empirical models built solely on theory are unlikely to be statistically adequate. Empirical models can be used in one (or more) of four different roles: theory testing, prediction, measurement, and characterization. Empirical models are wholly unsuited to testing theoretical models, a point we make by demonstrating that testing a deductive theoretical model with deductive hypothesis tests is not logically possible (the approach to inference taken does not matter). We present examples of empirical models being used for measurement and characterization that also make the point that empirical models can be useful when not testing theory. Predictive empirical models, like predictive theoretical models, are rare in political science.

How to combine theoretical and empirical models in a justifiable way is our last topic. Explanation consists either of an argument showing that some phenomenon was to be expected or the specification of a causal mechanism. In either case, empirical models are unable to capture these notions, and thus are incapable of providing explanations. Theoretical models, however, can provide explanations. A solid justification for linking theoretical and empirical models is that the former can provide explanations for the latter. We show that it is possible to choose between explanations in a relative sense, but that choosing between explanations is often unnecessary.

7.3 ISSUES AND COUNTERARGUMENTS

Having built a more justifiable framework for the use and evaluation of both theoretical and empirical models, we turn to addressing questions raised by our arguments and raised about our arguments. The latter come from reviewers, conferences, and colleagues. Undoubtedly, other critiques will emerge, and we welcome a constructive debate about the future of the discipline. It has been a long time coming.

We address eight issues:

- Talking about these issues is a distraction from "getting on with our work."
- I believe your arguments, but I will be criticized for adopting them.

- You make an analogy between models and maps, but maps are tested!
- Your approach to model evaluation is not precise.
- Perhaps proponents of EITM cannot show evidence of progress, but neither can you.
- What about verbal or computational models?
- What should a political scientist do differently when he or she sits down at the computer to work?
- Where do we go from here?

Talking about These Issues Is a Distraction from "Getting on with Our Work"

There is no separation between the work of political scientists and the issues raised in this book. Every referee who sends in a report arguing that a theoretical model is interesting but should not be published without a corresponding empirical test is staking out a philosophical position. Every researcher who equates a cause and an explanation is making a philosophical commitment. Every teacher who tells a class of graduate students that rational choice is not falsifiable is making a claim about what makes political science scientific. Debates about how to do political science are neither luxuries nor wastes of time. They are part and parcel of what we do.

Scholars who claim that we should "just get on with our work" and ignore philosophy of science often have the strongest and most inflexible views on the nature of "science." These views, whether or not these scholars realize it, depend heavily on a discredited philosophy of science (H-D or its variants). Unless the field updates its understanding of these issues, advisers will continue to transmit these outdated ideas to graduate students. Although many political scientists view philosophy of science as a sideshow, it is central to what we do, and being aware of developments in this area is as important for the discipline as staying current in economics, statistics, game theory, or history.

The well-justified methodological position that we have articulated provides valuable offense against those who try to impose a narrow (and we believe unsupportable) view about the role of models in our discipline. Rather than allow anti–rational choice scholars such as Green and Shapiro to define the debate in purely H-D terms, a formal modeler can point out that their argument hinges on an specious conception of scientific inquiry. Arguing that Green and Shapiro's critiques of rational choice are beside the point is a stronger position than arguing that rational choice theories are rigorously tested.

I Believe Your Arguments, but I Will Be Criticized for Adopting Them

At the risk of being repetitive, our book provides defenses against several common claims.

- *There is an agreed upon "scientific method" that exists in the hard sciences which political scientists should emulate.* The "scientific method" described in most textbooks is H-D, but scholars who study the hard sciences reject the claim that scientists follow this or any other method. We provide numerous cites to work that criticizes the H-D method.
- *Current practice is philosophy-free.* Current practice is deeply rooted in H-D, which is viewed as so obviously correct that debates about how science should be practiced, to the extent such debates exist, concern operating with the H-D framework. We provide strong evidence that the field thinks in terms of H-D and that H-D has philosophical roots.
- *It is possible to falsify a theoretical model with an empirical test.* We make three arguments relevant to this point. First, scholars who study models almost universally agree that models are objects, and thus are incapable of being true or false. Second, no theoretical model contains only true assumptions, so the truth status of a derived implication is uninformative regarding the truth status of the model. Third, theoretical models are not tested with data; they are tested with models of data. If a theoretical model is deemed false by the H-D method, the fault

could lie anywhere (the theoretical model, the empirical model, the data, statistical science, etc.).

- *Theoretical models must be tested empirically to be useful.* We discuss and provide examples of three kinds of theoretical models that can be useful without being tested: foundational models, organizational models, and exploratory models. (Predictive models are part of our discussion of H-D in chapter 2.) Theoretical modelers still face the burden of demonstrating that others should care about their model.

- *Empirical models must be derived from theoretical models to be useful.* We show that empirical models are not simply theoretical models with error terms, but must draw on information that can only come from the data. In addition, empirical models often must include variables that do not appear in the theoretical model (theory is general; data are specific).

- *The primary purpose of empirical models is to test theoretical models.* We discuss and provide examples of two uses of empirical models that do not require testing: measurement and characterization. Predictive models are rarely used in political science, and empirical models are not useful for testing theoretical models (as discussed in chapters 2 and 5).

- *Theory testing is the only way to unite theoretical and empirical models.* We make two arguments regarding this claim. First, we show that deductive theory testing cannot unite theoretical and empirical models, for reasons already discussed. Second, we suggest that the construction of explanations can unite theoretical and empirical models. The latter cannot serve as explanations on their own; they require theoretical models to provide the necessary argument or mechanism for which explanations call.

- *To identify a cause is to provide an explanation.* Explanations come in two forms: arguments and mechanisms. In neither case is it sufficient simply to determine a cause. Thus, empirical models that claim to determine causation, such as matching models, still require a theoretical model before a claim to explanation can be made.

These assertions have important consequences, as they inform the decisions of reviewers, editors, and publishers and therefore shape the trajectory of the field and the incentives of researchers who must "publish or perish." Our replies and our perspective on models in general allow researchers to justify their work on appropriate grounds, rather than forcing it into the dominant H-D perspective. We argued in chapter 4, for instance, that the analytic narratives methodology is weakened by characterizing it in terms of model "testing," when the approach seems best suited for using theoretical models to better understand specific events (i.e., as "exploratory models," in our categorization). Scholars who fail to update in a timely fashion risk their work being viewed as outdated.

You Make an Analogy between Models and Maps, but Maps Are Tested!

One of the most frequently made comments regarding our argument is that the maps analogy we use throughout the book is flawed in a particular way. We use the maps analogy to make the points that models are objects, have limited accuracy, are partial, and are purpose-relative. If we adopt this view of models, then it makes no sense to test them. Every map is "true" and "false" in an almost infinite number of ways (infinite because our world is infinitely complex). Simply deriving one or more hypotheses from a map and testing them is nonsensical. Some will hold, and some will not, and none of these results directly addresses how useful the map is. A map is a representation of reality, not reality itself. Maps reduce the three-dimensional world into two dimensions, and the reduction is necessarily accompanied by distortion. The same is true of models.

The objection is that maps are tested. That is, the objection presumes that before a subway map is released to the public, for example, it is given to a few people to try. The presumption may well be true—neither of us work for a transport authority—but if it is, it is a point in our favor. The subway map is being evaluated for its usefulness for a particular purpose (navigating the subway system). This approach is precisely the one we should take with models. Theoretical models can be foundational, organizational, exploratory, and predictive, and their evaluation should focus on these specific uses rather than focusing on testing a handful of deduced hypotheses. As long as the "testing" or evaluation occurs within the specified use, then the evaluation is justified.

The difference between H-D testing and usefulness evaluation is not a matter of semantics. Model testing in political science is rooted in a philosophy that views testing as central to the scientific enterprise. This approach has implications for the kinds of models that are constructed, the kinds of questions that drive research, and the kinds of data that are collected. In the end, what we call evaluating a model for its usefulness is unimportant provided that we think about and use models in a way that is consistent with their nature.[1]

Your Approach to Model Evaluation Is Not Precise

This point is on the mark, although not as a criticism. We have indeed traded the illusion of precise standards for better grounded but perhaps more vague criteria. In doing so, we are simply returning to an earlier time in the history of political science. Morris Fiorina, a pioneer in the use of models to study politics, put it best: "Judge work involving models as one would judge any other work. Is it careful, insightful, and does it advance our understanding? In the end every study must be judged against those standards" (Fiorina 1975, 154). There is no mystery regarding the evaluation of models, but neither is there a recipe. Model evaluation calls for judgment, and judgment comes with knowledge and experience.

In chapter 4, as a way of facilitating good judgment, we discuss a series of questions that a researcher might think through when making arguments in favor of her theoretical model. These questions are inextricably linked to the use for which the model was designed.

The function of a model creates its own metric of success. In chapter 5, we discuss empirical models and argue that the primary goal of empirical modeling must be statistical adequacy. The deductive nature of statistical learning demands it. We also show that of the many functions for which statistical models can be used, theory testing is not among them. In chapter 6, we show how competing empirical models and their associated explanations can be compared relative to one another. Even here, though, concluding that one explanation is superior to another is not to say that either explanation is interesting or true or worthy of additional study. Moreover, in many cases, comparing competing explanations is not necessary because the explanations answer different questions or describe different parts of a complex whole or because they all add valuable insight.

Ultimately, there is no escaping Fiorina's point. Model evaluation is not a matter of statistical tests and significance; it is a matter of recognizing when a model contributes to our collective understanding of politics.

Proponents of EITM Cannot Show Evidence that Their Methodology Has Led to Progress, but Neither Can You

Fair enough. On the other hand, we are also not trying to restrict the definition of good work in political science to a theoretical model tested by an empirical model (or their verbal equivalents). Theoretical and empirical models can perform a number of different functions beyond the generation and testing of hypotheses, and progress is not going to result from artificially suppressing this variety. We should encourage scholars to make contributions in their areas of strength, either in theory or empirics, and not let their imaginations be constrained by testing concerns. Invaluable insights came from Arrow, Dahl, Fenno, Kaplan, Key, Morgenthau, Olson, Sartori, Singer, Waltz, Wilson, and many others without concern for the issues that animate the EITM movement.[2]

More broadly, judging progress in political science is a tricky business. In other scientific endeavors, there often exists an external source through which progress can be measured. The fact that people generally live longer and healthier lives serves as such a measure for medicine. Chemists and engineers produce better and safer plastics and smaller and faster computers. Microbiologists make measurable progress against pestilence and disease. Oceanographers and meteorologists add precious seconds to tsunami and tornado warnings. Political science has few such external measures. In cases where there is nearly universal agreement on what constitutes progress—fewer instances of genocide—political science is unlikely to play a major (or any) role. In most cases, however, it is unclear what "better" means as politics involves inherently conflictual situations. "Better" for which side? "Better" in a vague general sense? Or "better" in a specific normative sense (e.g., Pareto optimality), which itself might be the subject of dispute? There is no single correct answer to these questions. Progress in political science is best measured by understanding, and understanding is not produced by using regressions to test the deductive implications of a theoretical model.

What about Qualitative or Computational Models?

Political science, like many social sciences, is becoming increasingly technical, and with that increased proficiency comes a tendency to equate modeling with mathematics. Many of the examples in this book are of mathematical models, primarily game theoretic or statistical in nature, in part to reflect the ubiquity of these techniques in the discipline and in part because those are the areas of the discipline that we know best. Many political science models, however, are neither games nor regressions; many are not even mathematical. The models being tested in Hopf (1991) are decidedly nonmathematical (neorealism and the offense-defense balance), and the evidence amassed is mostly qualitative. H-D suffuses the predictions and tests in Hopf's work as much as it does the work of any of the quantitative scholars cited in chapter 2. Similarly, Pahre (2005, 138) argues that "case studies can contribute to research designs for formal theorists testing their claims." Thus, our arguments lose none of their power when moved to a qualitative setting. We can discuss the similarities and dissimilarities between these models and the real world, the purposes for which these models are intended and how well they achieve those purposes, and whether the models generate significant insights.[3]

As for computational models, a recent paper by Kollman (2011) has a viewpoint similar to ours. Kollman focuses on models that "tell a narrative for how some process works but with the assumptions about the intentions of the actors and the processes of interactions specified precisely" (4), which we call theoretical models. He argues that models serve different purposes, which differ slightly from ours (models can be used to predict, gain conceptual clarity, and lend insight). He rejects a focus on prediction, arguing that better predictions often come at the expense of insights into why patterns emerge.[4] He argues that theoretical models (and computational models) can serve as explanations in the same way that we argue theoretical models can.

Kollman's arguments in favor of computational models focus on the notion of use. For example, he notes that not all computational models have an equilibrium, which is one of the main differences between traditional formal models and computational models. He argues, however, that equilibrium analysis is not the main purpose of computational models. Rather, the analysis of dynamics is the main purpose:

> Computational models demonstrate evolutions of processes, not assumptions that describe equilibrium outcomes. The analysis of dynamics is often the main *purpose* of using computational models. Acceptable or not to critics, the main defense of these models is that the modelers see dynamics in the real world, and equilibrium models cannot do justice as explanations of those dynamics.
>
> (Kollman 2011, 29)

Arguing for a model based on use, rather than its predictive capabilities, is precisely the kind of change for which we advocate.

What Should a Political Scientist Do Differently When He or She Sits Down at the Computer to Work?

This question (or some variant of it) has been asked by numerous academic readers at all career stages. The question sometimes takes the form, "What research gets done that shouldn't as a result of the current emphasis on model testing?" or "What research doesn't get done that should?" Finally, we are sometimes asked, "Why are you spending time on this project instead of doing 'real' research?"

The last question is the easiest to answer: we firmly believe that ideas about what constitutes "good work" have real consequences for the kinds of research that is publishable. After all, the decision of the *American Journal of Political Science* a few years back to insist that theoretical models be accompanied by empirical tests was not a brainstorm had by the editors but a response to reviewer demands. The expectation is that empirical models will be used to test theoretical models, and that theoretical models will be tested. Space in the discipline must be made before more work that flouts these norms can get through peer review. We hope that this book creates that space.

The other questions need to be addressed more carefully. The answer to the original question, "What should a political scientist do differently when he or she sits down at the computer to work?" is "Nothing, immediately." It is unlikely that practicing political scientists will abandon research agendas, rework existing papers, or otherwise change their mode of research based on our arguments. Our impact, we hope, will be in the long run. If we can encourage scholars to think differently about models, the purposes of models, and the interactions between models, then change will occur over time. Authors will begin to specify the purposes of the models in their work, and reviewers will drop demands that all theoretical models be tested. In this way, slowly but surely change will take place.

We suspect that this book will have its greatest impact in "scope and methods"–type courses in graduate schools. The earlier that graduate students can begin to think about these issues and work through the logic of H-D testing for themselves, the better. These students will go on to review each other's papers and take a broader view of what constitutes good work. In time, the spell that theoretical model testing holds over the discipline will be broken.

Where Do We Go from Here?

Models are central to the enterprise of political science, and we have laid out a model-based view of science that challenges the current orthodoxy (H-D theory testing). We have shown that the H-D approach simply does not do what it claims, and our alternative methodology is a firmer foundation upon which to build the discipline. As we promised, we did not provide a cookbook for doing political science, and we make no apologies for that. We hope our book spurs renewed discussion about the use of models in the discipline. Additionally, we hope this volume spurs additional thinking about these issues and that others can improve on what we have started.

The phrase "ideas have consequences" may be trite, but it nonetheless applies here. The ideas of William Riker, which built on the ideas of the day's leading philosophers of science, still have enormous currency in the discipline as it struggles to do Science with a capital "S." We hope to spur a vigorous debate and ultimately a new direction for the discipline: one that embraces the informed use of models to further our understanding of the political world.

CHAPTER 1
The epigraph is from Hoover (1995, 733).

1. We do not mean to imply that all of political science concerns models. Normative theory is one example of an area where models are less central.
2. "*S* uses *X* to represent *W* for purposes *P*" (Giere 2006, 60).
3. Any emphasis is from the original source in all quoted material throughout the book, unless otherwise noted.
4. We do not, however, argue that models are fictions.
5. The falsifiability criterion only states that a claim be refutable; any claim that can be tested, however nonsensical, cannot be pseudo-scientific.
6. Green and Shapiro (1994) is the rare political science book that includes discussions of issues in the philosophy of science.
7. Most scholars are aware of the old saw attributed to George Box that "all models are wrong, but some are useful."

CHAPTER 2
The epigraph is from Kyburg (1988, 61).

1. To be coded as practicing the method, authors had to either (1) derive, formally or not, testable hypotheses from a model or theory and then make claims about the state of the model or theory based on the outcomes of those tests; or (2) make a statement that model testing *should* be accomplished by testing hypotheses derived from the model. Political philosophy articles were excluded from the sample. An independent research assistant classified 65 percent of the sample as using the method, and nearly 40 percent of the sample was classified independently as using the method by both the authors and the research assistant.

2. "Prediction" here is being used in its broad sense to mean any deductive implication of the theory.

3. A logically valid argument is one where if the premises are true, then the conclusion must be true.

4. In the discussion to follow, we make use of the following symbols from first-order predicate logic. *Implication*: The symbol for implication is the arrow, $\rightarrow$, which stands for an "if ... then" statement. $A \rightarrow B$ is read as "If A is true, then B is true." We use the implication symbol to make statements such as "If some theory is true, then some hypothesis should hold" or $T \rightarrow H$. *Negation*: the symbol for negation is $\neg$. $\neg A$ stands for "A is false" or "not A" or "it is not the case that A." We use negation to stand for the falsity of a theory or hypothesis, $\neg T$ or $\neg H$. *Logical validity*: The symbol $\vdash$ means "is logically valid" or "therefore" (Lemmon 1992). If we assume $A \rightarrow B$ and A, then we can logically conclude B. A valid deduction, then, takes the form $A \rightarrow B, A \vdash B$. If the deduction is not valid, we use $\nvdash$, $A \rightarrow B, B \nvdash A$. If we assume $A \rightarrow B$ and B, then we cannot logically conclude A.

5. There exist differences between Fisherian hypothesis testing and Neyman-Pearson hypothesis testing (see Howson and Urbach 1993). These differences, however, do not affect our argument.

6. There is an exception to this rule. If the premise p is false, then the implication $p \rightarrow q$ is trivially true.

7. We thank Jim Snyder for bringing the rounding of constants to our attention.

8. For example, see Cross (1982) for a detailed examination of the many auxiliary hypotheses involved in testing macroeconomic theories.

9. The analytic/synthetic distinction is called into question by Quine (1951).

10. We are eliding somewhat the distinctions that exist between logical positivism and logical empiricism as well as the distinctions within these groups over time. Much of the Received View can be attributed to the logical empiricists Carl Hempel and Ernest Nagel after the heyday of logical positivism. Nonetheless, the Received View is a product of logical positivism (Suppe 1977).

11. A statistical version of the deductive-nomological model called the inductive-statistical model is also under the "covering model" rubric (Suppe 1977, 619). Distinguishing the two adds little to the point that we are making.

CHAPTER 3

The epigraph is from Carroll (1893, 169).

1. To be specific, maps are tools that work in a particular way: by representing. In this way, models are more akin to maps than to other sorts of tools, such as hammers.

2. Although the semantic and predicate views are theoretically distinct, the two terms are often used interchangeably in practice with little harm. In both approaches, models are nonlinguistic entities. We use the term "semantic."

3. We are eliding, as in the previous chapter, the difference between the logical positivists and the logical empiricists.

4. A set of sentences is fully interpreted if all the sentences have meanings that make them either true or false.

5. The Received View changed in both subtle and not-so-subtle ways over the years. This characterization is close to the final version.

6. The authors rely on survey data from the 1952, 1956, and 1960 presidential elections.

7. The authors assume that C is weakly negatively correlated with D and is constant within categories of D.

8. Most scholars date the death of the Received View to the opening night of the Illinois Symposium on the Structure of Scientific Theories, March 26, 1969 (Suppe 2000, S102).

9. See Suppe (1977) for a complete account of the rise and fall of the Received View.

10. Van Fraassen (1980, 41–43) uses the Seven Point Geometry as an example. If theory T includes the axioms: A0: There is at least one line; A1: For any two lines, there is at most one point that lies on both; A2: For any two points, there is exactly one line that lies on both; A3: On every line there lie at least two points; A4: There are only finitely many points; then, the Seven Point Geometry is a model of T because all five axioms are true in the structure.

11. Van Fraassen (1972, 312) provides an example. "Let the states of a classical particle moving along a straight line be represented by triples of real numbers, such that the particle is in state $< m, x, v >$ at time t exactly if it has mass m, position x, and velocity v at that time. Then if U is the statement that the kinetic energy equals e, we have $h(U) = \{< m, x, v >: \frac{1}{2} mv^2 = e\}$. This defines the set of states that satisfy U; U is true when related to a given system exactly if that system is in a state belonging to $h(U)$."

12. There is always the possibility of "internal falsification" stemming from errors in reasoning or mathematics. Such a statement is very different from the claim that a model is false.

13. The authors also consider extensions that demonstrate conditions under which inequities among states can arise.

Chapter 4

The epigraph is from Aumann (1985, 37).

1. Theoretical models, unlike statistical models, can achieve a purpose independent of data. Still, many theoretical models are *empirically motivated* in that

they are inspired by a real-world puzzle or are designed to inform how one thinks about an empirical question.

2. Of course, not all models rely on deductive reasoning. Computational models are one example.

3. Binmore (1990) makes a similar point regarding how to classify game theoretic models.

4. Our categorization is similar in spirit to Apostel (1961), who categorizes models by aims: theory formation, simplification, reduction, extension, adequation, explanation, concretization, globalization, action, and experimentation. Our categorization is more compact, but our categories subsume many of the aims mentioned by Apostel.

5. In Clarke and Primo (2007), we propose an additional category: generative models. The purpose of these models is to generate interesting and nonobvious statements about the phenomenon under study. In many ways, though, this standard ought to apply to all models. In addition, we initially used the phrase "structural models" to refer to organizational models. However, because this term has a very different meaning in econometrics, we use "organizational models" in this book.

6. Arrow's Theorem also spawned a large normative literature asking which of his conditions ought to be relaxed, whether his conditions are normatively justified, and so on.

7. Even if the model did not provide new propositions, it would still be useful as an organizational model. Bueno de Mesquita et al. view their model as serving multiple purposes, especially prediction in the familiar hypothetico-deductivist vein.

8. This classification is a change from the categorization in Clarke and Primo (2007).

9. Note that we might also think of these models as foundational models, but order matters. A model that spurs others to create subsidiary models is foundational; that same model written down after a set of related models has already been created is organizational.

10. "What if" questions are often rather loosely referred to in political science as "counterfactuals." For several applications from political science, see Tetlock and Belkin (1996a).

11. Certainly scholars may argue that the narratives are not *effective* in explaining single events. This critique is an assessment of usefulness, not of the enterprise itself.

12. See Binmore (2007) for a different perspective on this literature.

13. Of course, non–rational choice models yield refutable propositions, as well.

14. The same is true of sociology (see Gerber and Malhotra 2008b).

15. We inserted the word [not] into the quotation because it appears to have been inadvertently omitted from the original text of Aumann's work.

16. As Laver (1997, 6) notes, prediction is not the "be-all and end-all" of model evaluation. Elsewhere, Laver writes, "One reason for looking favourably upon precise predictions bears upon yet another criterion for evaluating models, which is their empirical accuracy. Models can, either directly or indirectly, be used to generate statements about the real world. These statements can then be evaluated in terms of their empirical validity.... *my own view is that the strict empirical accuracy of forecasts generated by any rational choice model is secondary to the value of the model in expanding our understanding of the world.* Nevertheless, other things being equal, it is obviously useful to construct at least some of our models on the basis of plausible, rather than implausible, assumptions. For this reason, we should not turn our backs on the empirical evaluation of propositions derived from our models" (7–8; emphasis added).

CHAPTER 5
The epigraph is from Lipkin (2000, 74).

1. Our use of Lipkin's quote should not be interpreted to mean that we view theory as unimportant. The quote's importance lies in the acknowledgment that empirical analysis can lead as opposed to follow.
2. A theoretical model maintains its generality even when applied to very specific circumstances.
3. Fixed effects are one example.
4. Formal theory is, of course, also dependent on the developmental state of formal theory. The difference lies in the dependence of empirical models on data *and* the state of statistical science.
5. More specifically, "We restrict ourselves to the simple case in which the data is an element of a real linear space Λ. The model Ω is a subset of Λ. The interpretation of the model is that $\eta \in \Omega$, where η is some idealized version of the actual observations y" (de Leeuw 1990).
6. The probability model is represented by $\Phi = \{f(x; \theta), \theta \in \Theta, x \in \mathbb{R}_X\}$, where Φ is a collection of density functions, one for each possible value of θ in the parameter space Θ.
7. A random sample is represented by $\mathbf{X} := (X_1, X_2, \dots, X_n)$.
8. The statistical generating mechanism is the orthogonal decomposition of the dependent variable into a systematic component and a nonsystematic component, $Y = E[Y|\mathcal{D}] + \mu$, where $\mathcal{D}$ is the conditioning information set (Spanos 1999, 370).
9.

$$\Phi = \{f(y_i|x_i; \theta) = \frac{1}{\sigma\sqrt{2}} \exp\left\{-\frac{(y_i - \beta_0 - \beta_1 x_i)^2}{2\sigma^2}\right\}, \theta \in \Theta, y_i \in \mathbb{R}\},$$

$$\boldsymbol{\theta} : (\beta_0, \beta_1, \sigma^2), \boldsymbol{\Theta} := \mathbb{R}^2 \times \mathbb{R}_+.$$

10. Some assumptions, such as the exogeneity of the right-hand-side variables, can only be tested indirectly.

11. In another paper, de Leeuw (1990) cites Ljung (1987, 6): "The question of nature's susceptibility to mathematical description has some deep philosophical aspects, and in practical terms we have to take a more pragmatic view of models. Our acceptance of models should thus be guided by 'usefulness' rather than 'truth.'"

12. Technically speaking, these variables are in the model; they are captured by the disturbance term, ϵ_i. How and whether omitted variables affect the results of an empirical model depends on a number of factors. See Clarke (2009) for additional information.

13. Other uses of empirical models exist. Political methodologists, for example, make use of models to demonstrate the utility of particular econometric methods.

14. The journals are *American Political Science Review, American Journal of Political Science*, and *Journal of Politics*.

15. The null hypothesis implies that the probability of the data, given that the null hypothesis is true, is large.

16. The following is a simple example of the fallacy.

$$\left.\begin{array}{l} \text{If } x \text{ is human, then } x \text{ is mortal,} \\ \qquad\qquad\qquad x \text{ is mortal} \end{array}\right\} \nvdash x \text{ is human.}$$

Despite the fact that x is mortal, we cannot conclude that x is human.

17. There is a temptation to combine the first deduction from the verificationist case, $TM \rightarrow H_1$, with the second deduction from the falsificationist logic, $H_0 \rightarrow P(y|H_0)$ is large. This strategy is not feasible, however. The premises in the final step would be $TM \rightarrow H_1$ and $\neg H_0$, and even if we could equate the truth of H_1 with the falsity of the null hypothesis, $H_1 \equiv \neg H_0$, we would be back in the same position of affirming the consequent, $TM \rightarrow H_1, H_1 \nvdash TM$.

18. See Barnett (1982) for a discussion of the benefits of Bayesianism.

19. There is a second Bayesian logic that is inductive. Given an inclusive set of theories, Bayesian methods could be used to pick the theory most supported by the data. This formulation is also problematic. See Clarke (2007a) for an analysis.

20. A structural model posits an *a priori* ordering of the variables in a data set in accord with hypothesized cause-and-effect relationships (Cameron and Trivedi 2005). As noted earlier in the chapter, theory can often be useful in identifying such models.

21.   The approach used to model senators is similar, except it rules out running for a different office.

CHAPTER 6
The epigraph is from Hempel and Oppenheim (1948, 135).

1.   Our claim here is not that using a map to help construct a second map is the *only* way to construct the second map; the claim is that the first map can be helpful in such an endeavor.

2.   Aldrich's (1980, 4) early statement calling for the linking of theoretical and empirical models is worth quoting in full:

> Empirical observation, in the absence of a theoretical base, is at best descriptive. It tells one what has happened, but not why it has the pattern one perceives. Theoretical analysis, in the absence of empirical testing, has a framework more noteworthy for its logical or mathematical elegance than for its utility in generating insights into the real world. The first exercise has been described as "data dredging," the second as building "irrelevant models of irrelevant universes." My purpose is to try to understand what I believe to be a problem of major importance. This understanding cannot be achieved merely by observation, nor can it be attained by the manipulation of abstract symbols. Real insight can be gained only by their combination.

3.   The problem arises from the observation that no theory is tested in isolation. It is impossible to falsify a theory or hypothesis because we cannot be sure whether the main hypothesis, one or more auxiliary hypotheses, a *ceteris paribus* clause, or a boundary condition is false.

4.   A possible exception is empirical models that seek to determine facts and answer policy questions.

5.   Brady (2004a) calls for a more ecumenical view of explanation, one that admits causality but also considers (if not accepts) as explanations classification systems, like those in biology.

6.   Loosely speaking, two events are constantly conjoined if whenever one occurs the other one also occurs.

7.   Pevehouse also discusses why democracies in regional organizations have an incentive to democratize others in the group.

8.   Pevehouse (2002, 531) claims to be "testing" his argument by examining whether involvement in regional organizations is associated with democratization. It is more useful, for the reasons discussed in this book, to think of Pevehouse as providing an explanation for the statistical relationship that he identifies.

9. Elster (2007, 32) refers to similar sequences of events as "causal chains."

10. See Gerber and Green (2000, 655) for the details of their $2 \times 2 \times 4$ study design.

11. This article spawned a vigorous debate about the role of committees in legislatures (see Krehbiel, Shepsle, and Weingast 1987 for an early debate).

12. Shepsle and Weingast do not provide specific conditions under which proposals are made.

13. There are many situations in which rival explanations either do not need to be compared empirically or it is illogical to compare them or both. We discuss these situations following our discussion of comparative model testing.

CHAPTER 7

The epigraph is from Theil (1971, iv).

1. On a humorous note, graduate students at the University of Rochester have begun using air quotes when saying the word *testing* in seminars with the authors. Whether this is done to mock or express solidarity with the authors is unclear.

2. We do not mean to imply that the empiricists in the group never thought about models or that the theorists never thought about data. Their most important insights, however, were not the product of combining theoretical and empirical models.

3. Pahre (2005, 138) also notes that "formal theory and qualitative methods share many epistemological precepts."

4. See de Marchi (2005) for another perspective on computational modeling.

BIBLIOGRAPHY

Acemoglu, Daron, and James A. Robinson. 2006. *Economic Origins of Dictatorship and Democracy*. New York: Cambridge University Press.

Achen, Christopher H. 1982. *Interpreting and Using Regression*. Thousand Oaks, CA: Sage.

Achen, Christopher H. 1983. "Toward Theories of Data: The State of Political Methodology." In *Political Science: The State of the Discipline*, ed. Ada W. Finifter. Washington, DC: American Political Science Association.

Achen, Christopher H. 1992. "Social Psychology, Demographic Variables, and Linear Regression: Breaking the Iron Triangle in Voting Research." *Political Behavior* 14 (3): 195–211.

Achen, Christopher H. 2002. "Microfoundations and ART." *Annual Review of Political Science* 5: 423–50.

Achen, Christopher H., and Larry M. Bartels. 2004. "Blind Retrospection: Electoral Responses to Drought, Flu, and Shark Attacks." Working Paper, Princeton Univeristy.

Aldrich, John H. 1980. *Before the Convention: Strategies and Choices in Presidential Nomination Campaigns*. Chicago: University of Chicago Press.

Aldrich, John, and James Alt. 2003. "Introduction to the Special Issue." *Political Analysis* 11 (4): 309–15.

Aldrich, John, James E. Alt, and Arthur Lupia. 2007. "The EITM Approach: Origins and Interpretations." In *Oxford Handbook of Political Methodology*, ed. Janet Box-Steffensmeier, Henry Brady, and David Collier. New York: Oxford University Press.

Allison, Graham T. 1971. *Essence of Decision: Explaining the Cuban Missile Crisis*. Glenview, IL: Scott, Foresman.

Alvarez, R. Michael, and Lisa García Bedolla. 2003. "The Foundations of Latino Voter Partisanship: Evidence from the 2000 Election." *Journal of Politics* 65 (1): 31–49.

Andreoni, James, and John H. Miller. 1993. "Rational Cooperation in the Finitely Repeated Prisoner's Dilemma: Experimental Evidence." *Economic Journal* 103 (418): 570–85.

Ansolabehere, Stephen, James M. Snyder Jr., and Michael M. Ting. 2003. "Bargaining in Bicameral Legislatures: When and Why Does Malapportionment Matter?" *American Political Science Review* 97 (3): 471–81.

Apostel, Leo. 1961. "Towards the Formal Study of Models in the Non-formal Sciences." In *The Concept and the Role of the Model in Mathematics and Natural and Social Sciences*, ed. Hans Freudenthal. Dordrecht, Holland: Reidel.

Arrow, Kenneth J. 1963. *Social Choice and Individual Values*, 2nd ed. New York: Wiley.

Aumann, Robert J. 1985. "What Is Game Theory Trying to Accomplish?" In *Frontiers of Economics*, ed. Kenneth J. Arrow and Seppo Honkapohja. Oxford: Basil Blackwell.

Austen-Smith, David, and Jeffrey S. Banks. 1998. "Social Choice Theory, Game Theory, and Positive Political Theory." *Annual Review of Political Science* 1: 259–87.

Bailer-Jones, Daniela M. 2009. *Scientific Models in Philosophy of Science*. Pittsburgh: University of Pittsburgh Press.

Banks, Jeffrey S., and John Duggan. 2000. "A Bargaining Model of Collective Choice." *American Political Science Review* 94 (1): 73–88.

Barnett, Vic. 1982. *Comparative Statistical Inference*, 2nd ed. New York: Wiley.

Baron, David P. 1991. "A Spatial Bargaining Theory of Government Formation in Parliamentary Systems." *American Political Science Review* 85 (1): 137–64.

Baron, David P., and John A. Ferejohn. 1989. "Bargaining in Legislatures." *American Political Science Review* 83 (4): 1181–206.

Bartels, Larry, and Henry E. Brady. 1993. "The State of Quantitative Political Methodology." In *Political Science: The State of the Discipline II*, ed. Ada W. Finifter. Washington, DC: American Political Science Association.

Bates, Robert H. 2008. *When Things Fell Apart: State Failure in Late-Century Africa*. New York: Cambridge University Press.

Bates, Robert H., Avner Greif, Margaret Levi, Jean-Laurent Rosenthal, and Barry R. Weingast. 1998. *Analytic Narratives*. Princeton: Princeton University Press.

Bates, Robert H., Avner Greif, Margaret Levi, Jean-Laurent Rosenthal, and Barry R. Weingast. 2000. "The Analytic Narrative Project." *American Political Science Review* 94 (3): 696–702.

Battaglini, Marco, and Stephen Coate. 2007. "Inefficiency in Legislative Policymaking: A Dynamic Analysis." *American Economic Review* 97 (1): 118–49.

Baumol, William J., and Alan S. Blinder. 2009. *Economics: Principles and Policy*, 11th ed. Mason, OH: South-Western Cengage Learning.

Bell, Duncan. 2008. *Political Thought and International Relations: Variations on a Realist Theme*. New York: Oxford University Press.

Bendor, Jonathan, and Adam Meirowitz. 2004. "Spatial Models of Delegation." *American Political Science Review* 98 (2): 293–310.

Berk, Richard A. 2004. *Regression Analysis: A Constructive Critique*. Thousand Oaks, CA: Sage.

Berrebi, Claude, and Esteban F. Klor. 2008. "Are Voters Sensitive to Terrorism? Direct Evidence from the Israeli Electorate." *American Political Science Review* 102 (3): 279–301.

Berry, Christopher R. 2009. *Imperfect Union: Representation and Taxation in Multilevel Governments*. New York: Cambridge University Press.

Binmore, Ken G. 1990. *Essays on the Foundations of Game Theory*. Cambridge, MA: Basil Blackwell.

Binmore, Ken G. 2007. *Does Game Theory Work? The Bargaining Challenge*. Cambridge, MA: MIT Press.

Black, Duncan. 1958. *The Theory of Committees and Elections*. Cambridge: Cambridge University Press.

Black, Max. 1962. *Models and Metaphors: Studies in Language and Philosophy*. Ithaca, NY: Cornell University Press.

Blaug, Mark. 1992. *The Methodology of Economics: Or How Economists Explain*, 2nd ed. New York: Cambridge University Press.

Boyd, Richard, Philip Gasper, and J. D. Trout, eds. 1993. *The Philosophy of Science*. Cambridge, MA: MIT Press.

Brady, Henry E. 2004a. "Doing Good and Doing Better: How Far Does the Quantitative Template Get Us?" In *Rethinking Social Inquiry*, ed. Henry E. Brady and David Collier. Lanham, MD: Rowman and Littlefield.

Brady, Henry E. 2004b. "Introduction to Symposium: Two Paths to a Science of Politics." *Perspectives on Politics* 2 (2): 295–300.

Brady, Henry E., and David Collier, eds. 2004. *Rethinking Social Inquiry*. Lanham, MD: Rowman and Littlefield.

Braumoeller, Bear F., and Anne E. Sartori. 2004. "The Promise and Perils of Statistics in International Relations." In *Models, Numbers, and Cases: Methods for Studying International Relations*, ed. Detlef F. Sprinz and Yael Wolinsky-Nahmias. Ann Arbor: University of Michigan Press.

Buchanan, James M., and Gordon Tullock. 1962. *The Calculus of Consent: Logical Foundations of Constitutional Democracy.* Ann Arbor: University of Michigan Press.

Bueno de Mesquita, Bruce, and David Lalman. 1992. *War and Reason.* New Haven: Yale University Press.

Bueno de Mesquita, Bruce, and Kenneth Shepsle. 2001. "William Harrison Riker: 1920–1993. A Biographical Memoir." *Biographical Memoirs* 79: 1–22.

Bueno de Mesquita, Bruce, Alastair Smith, Randolph M. Siverson, and James D. Morrow. 2003. *The Logic of Political Survival.* Cambridge, MA: MIT Press.

Caldwell, Bruce J. 1988. "The Case for Pluralism." In *The Popperian Legacy in Economics,* ed. Neil de Marchi. Cambridge: Cambridge University Press.

Camerer, Colin F. 2003. *Behavioral Game Theory: Experiments in Strategic Interaction.* Princeton, NJ: Princeton University Press.

Cameron, A. Colin, and Pravin K. Trivedi. 2005. *Microeconometrics: Methods and Applications.* New York: Cambridge University Press.

Campbell, Norman R. 1920. *Physics: The Elements.* London: Cambridge University Press.

Carpenter, Daniel. 2000. "Commentary: What Is the Marginal Value of Analytic Narratives?" *Social Science History* 24 (4): 653–67.

Carpenter, Daniel, Susan I. Moffitt, Colin D. Moore, Ryan T. Rynbrandt, Michael M. Ting, Ian Yohai, and Evan James Zucker. 2010. "Early Entrant Protection in Approval Regulation: Theory and Evidence from FDA Drug Review." *Journal of Law, Economics, and Organization* 26 (3): 515–45.

Carroll, Lewis. 1893. *Sylvie and Bruno Concluded.* New York: Macmillan.

Carroll, Royce, and Gary W. Cox. 2007. "The Logic of Gamson's Law: Pre-election Coalitions and Portfolio Allocations." *American Journal of Political Science* 51 (2): 300–13.

Cartwright, Nancy. 1983. *How the Laws of Physics Lie.* New York: Oxford University Press.

Cartwright, Nancy. 1991. "Fables and Models." *Proceedings of the Aristotelian Society, Supplementary Volumes* 65: 55–66.

Chalmers, A. F. 1982. *What Is This Thing Called Science?* St. Lucia: University of Queensland Press.

Chari, V. V., Larry E. Jones, and Ramon Marimon. 1997. "The Economics of Split-Ticket Voting in Representative Democracies." *American Economic Review* 87 (5): 957–76.

Chong, Dennis. 1995. "Rational Choice Theory's Mysterious Rivals." *Critical Review* 9 (1 and 2): 37–57.

Clark, William Roberts, Matt Golder, and Sona Nadenichek Golder. 2008. *Principles of Comparative Politics.* Washington, DC: CQ Press.

Clark, William Roberts, and Mark Hallerberg. 2000. "Mobile Capital, Domestic Institutions, and Electorally Induced Monetary and Fiscal Policy." *American Political Science Review* 94 (2): 323–46.

Clarke, Kevin A. 2001. "Testing Nonnested Models of International Relations: Reevaluating Realism." *American Journal of Political Science* 45 (3): 724–44.

Clarke, Kevin A. 2002. "The Reverend and the Ravens." *Political Analysis* 10 (2): 194–97.

Clarke, Kevin A. 2007a. "The Necessity of Being Comparative: Theory Confirmation in Quantitative Political Science." *Comparative Political Studies* 40 (7): 886–908.

Clarke, Kevin A. 2007b. "A Simple Distribution-Free Test for Nonnested Hypotheses." *Political Analysis* 15 (3): 347–63.

Clarke, Kevin A. 2009. "Return of the Phantom Menace: Omitted Variable Bias in Econometric Research." *Conflict Management and Peace Science* 26 (1): 46–66.

Clarke, Kevin A., and David M. Primo. 2007. "Modernizing Political Science: A Model-Based Approach." *Perspectives on Politics* 5 (4): 741–53.

Clinton, Joshua, Simon Jackman, and Douglas Rivers. 2004. "The Statistical Analysis of Roll Call Data." *American Political Science Review* 98 (2): 355–70.

Coate, Stephen, and Michael Conlin. 2004. "A Group Rule-Utilitarian Approach to Voter Turnout: Theory and Evidence." *American Economic Review* 94 (5): 1476–504.

Coate, Stephen, Michael Conlin, and Andrea Moro. 2008. "The Performance of Pivotal-Voter Models in Small-Scale Elections: Evidence from Texas Liquor Referenda." *Journal of Public Economics* 92 (3–4): 582–96.

Contessa, Gabriele. 2009. "Review of Bas van Fraassen's 'Scientific Representation: Paradoxes of Perspective'." *Notre Dame Philosophical Reviews,* available online only.

Contessa, Gabriele. 2011. "Scientific Models and Representation." In *The Continuum Companion to the Philosophy of Science,* ed. Steven French and Juha Saatsi. London: Continuum.

Cooper, Russell, Douglas V. DeJong, Robert Forsythe, and Thomas W. Ross. 1996. "Cooperation without Reputation: Experimental Evidence from Prisoner's Dilemma Games." *Games and Economic Behavior* 12 (2): 187–218.

Cox, David R. 1961. "Tests of Separate Families of Hypotheses." *Proceedings of the Fourth Berkeley Symposium on Mathematical Statistics and Probability* I: 105–23.

Cox, Gary W. 1990. "Centripetal and Centrifugal Incentives in Electoral Systems." *American Journal of Political Science* 34 (4): 903–35.

Cross, Rod. 1982. "The Duhem-Quine Thesis, Lakatos, and the Appraisal of Theories in Macroeconomics." *Economic Journal* 92 (366): 320–40.

Dahl, Robert A. 1971. *Polyarchy: Participation and Opposition.* New Haven, CT: Yale University Press.

Davidson, Russell, and James G. MacKinnon. 1981. "Several Tests for Model Specification in the Presence of Alternative Hypotheses." *Econometrica* 49 (3): 781–93.

Dawes, Robyn M., and Richard H. Thaler. 1988. "Anomalies: Cooperation." *Journal of Economic Perspectives* 2 (3): 187–97.

de Leeuw, Jan. 1990. "Data Modeling and Theory Construction." In *Operationalization and Research Strategy*, ed. J. J. Hox and J. de Jong-Gierveld. Bristol, PA: Taylor and Francis.

de Leeuw, Jan. 1994. "Statistics and the Sciences." In *Trends and Perspectives in Empirical Social Research*, ed. Ingwer Borg and Peter Mohler. Berlin: Walter de Gruyter.

de Marchi, Scott. 2005. *Computational and Mathematical Modeling in the Social Sciences*. New York: Cambridge University Press.

Diermeier, Daniel. 1995. "Rational Choice and the Role of Theory in Political Science." *Critical Review* 9 (1 and 2): 59–70.

Diermeier, Daniel, and Timothy J. Feddersen. 1998. "Cohesion in Legislatures and the Vote of Confidence Procedure." *American Political Science Review* 92 (3): 611–21.

Diermeier, Daniel, Michael Keane, and Antonio Merlo. 2005. "A Political Economy Model of Congressional Careers." *American Economic Review* 95 (1): 347–73.

Doron, Gideon, and Itai Sened. 2001. *Political Bargaining: Theory, Practice and Process*. London: Sage.

Dowe, Phil. 2000. "Causality and Explanation." *British Journal for the Philosophy of Science* 51 (1): 165–74.

Downs, Anthony. 1957. *An Economic Theory of Democracy*. New York: Harper and Row.

Earman, John. 1992. *Bayes or Bust? A Critical Examination of Bayesian Confirmation Theory*. Cambridge, MA: MIT Press.

Easterly, William. 2001. *The Elusive Quest for Growth*. Cambridge, MA: MIT Press.

Elster, Jon. 2000. "Rational Choice History: A Case of Excessive Ambition." *American Political Science Review* 94 (3): 685–95.

Elster, Jon. 2007. *Explaining Social Behavior: More Nuts and Bolts for the Social Sciences*. New York: Cambridge University Press.

Epstein, Lee, and Jack Knight. 2002. "The Strategic John Marshall (and Thomas Jefferson)." In *Marbury versus Madison: Documents and Commentary*, ed. Mark A. Graber and Michael Perhac. Washington, DC: CQ Press.

Fearon, James D. 1995. "Rationalist Explanations for War." *International Organization* 49 (3): 379–414.

Fenno, Richard F. Jr. 1978. *Home Style: House Members in Their Districts*. Boston: Little, Brown.

Ferejohn, John, and Deborah Satz. 1995. "Unification, Universalism, and Rational Choice Theory." *Critical Review* 9(1 and 2): 71–84.

Fiorina, Morris P. 1975. "Formal Models in Political Science." *American Journal of Political Science* 19 (1): 133–59.

Fiorina, Morris P. 1995. "Rational Choice, Empirical Contributions, and the Scientific Enterprise." *Critical Review* 9 (1 and 2): 85–94.

Fowler, James. 2005. "Dynamic Responsiveness in the U.S. Senate." *American Journal of Political Science* 49 (2): 299–312.

Freedman, David, Robert Pisani, and Roger Purves. 1998. *Statistics*, 3rd ed. New York: Norton.

Friedman, Michael. 1974. "Explanation and Scientific Understanding." *Journal of Philosophy* 71 (1): 5–19.

Friedman, Milton. 1953. "The Methodology of Positive Economics." In *Essays in Positive Economics*, ed. Milton Friedman. Chicago: University of Chicago Press.

Friedman, Milton, and Anna J. Schwartz. 1991. "Alternative Approaches to Analyzing Economic Data." *American Economic Review* 81 (1): 39–49.

Fudenberg, Drew, and Jean Tirole. 1991. *Game Theory*. Cambridge, MA: MIT Press.

Geddes, Barbara. 2003. *Paradigms and Sand Castles: Theory Building and Research Design in Comparative Politics*. Ann Arbor: University of Michigan Press.

Gerber, Alan S., and Donald P. Green. 2000. "The Effects of Canvassing, Telephone Calls, and Direct Mail on Voter Turnout: A Field Experiment." *American Political Science Review* 94 (3): 653–63.

Gerber, Alan S., Donald P. Green, and David Nickerson. 2001. "Testing for Publication Bias in Political Science." *Political Analysis* 9 (4): 385–92.

Gerber, Alan S., and Neil Malhotra. 2008a. "Do Statistical Reporting Standards Affect What Is Published? Publication Bias in Two Leading Political Science Journals." *Quarterly Journal of Political Science* 3 (3): 313–26.

Gerber, Alan S., and Neil Malhotra. 2008b. "Publication Bias in Empirical Sociological Research: Do Arbitrary Significance Levels Distort Published Results?" *Sociological Methods & Research* 37 (1): 3–30.

Gerring, John. 2007. *Case Study Research: Principles and Practices*. New York: Cambridge University Press.

Gibbard, Allan. 1973. "Manipulation of Voting Schemes: A General Result." *Econometrica* 41 (4): 587–601.

Gibbard, Allan, and Hal R. Varian. 1978. "Economic Models." *Journal of Philosophy* 75 (11): 664–77.

Gibbons, Robert. 1992. *Game Theory for Applied Economists*. Princeton, NJ: Princeton University Press.

Giere, Ronald N. 1984. *Understanding Scientific Reasoning*, 2nd ed. New York: Holt, Rinehart, and Winston.

Giere, Ronald N. 1990. *Explaining Science: A Cognitive Approach*. Chicago: University of Chicago Press.

Giere, Ronald N. 1999. "Using Models to Represent Reality." In *Model-Based Reasoning in Scientific Discovery*, ed. Lorenzo Magnani, Nancy J. Nersessian, and Paul Thagard. New York: Kluwer Academic/Plenum.

Giere, Ronald N. 2006. *Scientific Perspectivism*. Chicago: University of Chicago Press.

Gill, Jeff. 2007. *Bayesian Methods: A Social and Behavioral Sciences Approach*, 2nd ed. New York: Chapman and Hall.

Glymour, Clark. 1980a. "Hypothetico-Deductivism Is Hopeless." *Philosophy of Science* 47 (2): 322–25.

Glymour, Clark. 1980b. *Theory and Evidence*. Princeton, NJ: Princeton University Press.

Godfrey-Smith, Peter. 2006. "The Strategy of Model-Based Science." *Biology and Philosophy* 21 (5): 725–40.

Godfrey-Smith, Peter. 2009. "Models and Fictions in Science." *Philosophical Studies* 143 (1): 101–16.

Goldthorpe, John H. 2001. "Causation, Statistics, and Sociology." *European Sociological Review* 17 (1): 1–20.

Goodman, Nelson. 1979. *Fact, Fiction, and Forecast*, 4th ed. Cambridge, MA: Harvard University Press.

Granato, Jim, Melody Lo, and M. C. Sunny Wong. 2010. "A Framework for Unifying Formal and Empirical Analysis." *American Journal of Political Science* 54 (3): 783–97.

Granato, Jim, and Frank Scioli. 2004. "Puzzles, Proverbs, and Omega Matrices: The Scientific and Social Significance of Empirical Implications of Theoretical Models (EITM)." *Perspectives on Politics* 2 (2): 313–23.

Green, Donald P., and Ian Shapiro. 1994. *Pathologies of Rational Choice Theory: A Critique of Applications in Political Science*. New Haven, CT: Yale University Press.

Green, Donald P., and Ian Shapiro. 1995. "Pathologies Revisited: Reflections On Our Critics." *Critical Review* 9 (1–2): 235–76.

Greene, William H. 2003. *Econometric Analysis*, 5th ed. New Jersey: Prentice Hall.

Grimes, Thomas R. 1990. "Truth, Content, and the Hypothetico-Deductive Method." *Philosophy of Science* 57 (3): 514–22.

Groseclose, Tim, and James M. Snyder Jr. 1996. "Buying Supermajorities." *American Political Science Review* 90 (2): 303–15.

Grossman, Gene M., and Elhanan Helpman. 1995. "Trade Wars and Trade Talks." *Journal of Political Economy* 103 (4): 675–708.

Haggett, Peter, and Richard J. Chorley. 1967. "Models, Paradigms, and the New Geography." In *Models in Geography*, ed. Richard J. Chorley and Peter Haggett. London: Methuen.

Hands, D. Wade. 2001. *Reflection without Rules: Economic Methodology and Contemporary Science Theory*. New York: Cambridge University Press.

Hanushek, Eric A., and John E. Jackson. 1977. *Statistical Methods for Social Scientists*. San Diego: Academic Press.

Hardin, Garrett. 1968. "The Tragedy of the Commons." *Science* 162 (3859): 1243–48.

Hausman, Daniel M. 1992. *The Inexact and Separate Science of Economics.* New York: Cambridge University Press.

Hausman, Daniel M. 1994. "Introduction." In *The Philosophy of Economics: An Anthology,* 2nd ed. New York: Cambridge University Press.

Helmke, Gretchen. 2005. *Courts under Constraints: Judges, Generals, and Presidents in Argentina.* New York: Cambridge University Press.

Hempel, Carl G. 1945. "Studies in the Logic of Confirmation." *Mind* 54: 1–26, 97–121.

Hempel, Carl G. 1962. "Explanation in Science and in History." In *Frontiers of Science and Philosophy,* ed. Robert G. Colodny. Pittsburgh, PA: University of Pittsburgh Press.

Hempel, Carl G., and Paul Oppenheim. 1948. "Studies in the Logic of Explanation." *Philosophy of Science* 15 (2): 135–75.

Herron, Michael C., and Jonathan Wand. 2007. "Assessing Partisan Bias in Voting Technology: The Case of the 2004 New Hampshire Recount." *Electoral Studies* 26 (2): 247–61.

Hesse, Mary B. 1966. *Models and Analogies in Science.* Notre Dame, IN: University of Notre Dame Press.

Hinich, Melvin J., and Michael C. Munger. 1997. *Analytical Politics.* New York: Cambridge University Press.

Hoover, Kevin D. 1995. "Review: Why Does Methodology Matter for Economics?" *Economic Journal* 105 (430): 715–34.

Hoover, Kevin D. 2006. "The Methodology of Econometrics." In *Palgrave Handbook of Econometrics: Econometric Theory,* ed. Terence C. Mills and Kerry Patterson. Vol. I. New York: Palgrave MacMillan.

Hopf, Ted. 1991. "Polarity, the Offense-Defense Balance, and War." *American Political Science Review* 85 (2): 475–93.

Howson, Colin, and Peter Urbach. 1993. *Scientific Reasoning: The Bayesian Approach,* 2nd ed. Chicago: Open Court.

Huth, Paul, Christopher Gelpi, and D. Scott Bennett. 1993. "The Escalation of Great Power Militarized Disputes: Testing Rational Deterrence Theory and Structural Realism." *American Political Science Review* 87 (3): 609–23.

Iversen, Torben, and David Soskice. 2006. "Electoral Institutions and the Politics of Coalitions: Why Some Democracies Redistribute More Than Others." *American Political Science Review* 100 (2): 165–81.

Johnson, James. 1996. "How Not to Criticize Rational Choice Theory: Pathologies of 'Common Sense'." *Philosophy of the Social Sciences* 26 (1): 77–91.

Johnson, James. 2006. "Consequences of Positivism: A Pragmatist Assessment." *Comparative Political Studies* 39 (2): 224–52.

Kahneman, Daniel, and Amos Tversky. 1979. "Prospect Theory: An Analysis of Decision under Risk." *Econometrica* 47 (2): 263–92.

King, Gary, Robert O. Keohane, and Sidney Verba. 1994. *Designing Social Inquiry: Scientific Inference and Qualitative Research*. Princeton, NJ: Princeton University Press.

Kitcher, Philip. 1981. "Explanatory Unification." *Philosophy of Science* 48 (4): 507–31.

Kitcher, Philip. 1989. "Explanatory Unification and the Causal Structure of the World." In *Scientific Explanation*, ed. Philip Kitcher and Wesley C. Salmon. Minneapolis: University of Minnesota Press.

Kollman, Ken. 2011. "The Potential Value of Computational Models in Social Science Research." Paper forthcoming in *The Oxford Handbook of the Philosophy of Social Science*, ed. Harold Kincaid. New York: Oxford University Press.

Kornhauser, Lewis A. 2009. "Modeling Courts." In *Theoretical Foundations of Law and Economics*, ed. Mark D. White. New York: Cambridge University Press.

Krehbiel, Keith. 1991. *Information and Legislative Organization*. Ann Arbor: University of Michigan Press.

Krehbiel, Keith. 1998. *Pivotal Politics: A Theory of U.S. Lawmaking*. Chicago: University of Chicago Press.

Krehbiel, Keith, Kenneth A. Shepsle, and Barry R. Weingast. 1987. "Why Are Congressional Committees Powerful?" *American Political Science Review* 81 (3): 929–45.

Kreps, David M. 1990. *Game Theory and Economic Modelling*. Oxford: Oxford University Press.

Kreps, David M., Paul Milgrom, John Roberts, and Robert Wilson. 1982. "Rational Cooperation in the Finitely Repeated Prisoners' Dilemma." *Journal of Economic Theory* 27 (2): 245–52.

Krueger, James S., and Michael S. Lewis-Beck. 2005. "The Place of Prediction in Politics." Paper presented at the annual meeting of the American Political Science Association.

Kuhn, T. S. 1970. *The Structure of Scientific Revolutions*, 2nd ed. Chicago: University of Chicago Press.

Kyburg, Henry E. Jr. 1988. "The Justification of Deduction in Science." In *The Limitations of Deductivism*, ed. Adolf Grünbaum and Wesley C. Salmon. Pittsburgh Series in Philosophy and History of Science. Berkeley: University of California Press.

Lakatos, Imre. 1970. "Falsification and the Methodology of Scientific Research Programs." In *Criticism and the Growth of Knowledge*, ed. Imre Lakatos and Alan Musgrave. Vol. 4 of *International Colloquium in the Philosophy of Science*. Cambridge: Cambridge University Press.

Lake, David A., and Matthew A. Baum. 2001. "The Invisible Hand of Democracy: Political Control and the Provision of Public Services." *Comparative Political Studies* 34 (6): 587–621.

Laudan, Larry. 1983. "The Demise of the Demarcation Problem." In *Physics, Philosophy and Psychoanalysis: Essays in Honor of Adolf Grunbaum*, ed. R. S. Cohen. Dordrecht, Holland: Reidel.

Laver, Michael. 1997. *Private Desires, Political Action: An Invitation to the Politics of Rational Choice*. Thousand Oaks, CA: Sage.

Lebow, Richard Ned, and Janice Gross Stein. 1996. "Back to the Past: Counterfactuals and the Cuban Missile Crisis." In *Counterfactual Thought Experiments in World Politics: Logical, Methodological, and Psychological Perspectives*, ed. Philip E. Tetlock and Aaron Belkin. Princeton, NJ: Princeton University Press.

Lemmon, E. J. 1992. *Beginning Logic*. Indianapolis: Hackett.

Leventoğlu, Bahar, and Ahmer Tarar. 2005. "Pre-negotiation Public Commitment in Domestic and International Bargaining." *American Political Science Review* 99 (3): 419–33.

Lieberson, Stanley. 1985. *Making it Count: The Improvement of Social Research and Theory*. Berkeley: University of California Press.

Lipkin, Harry J. 2000. "Who Ordered Theorists?" *Physics Today* 53 (7): 15, 74.

Little, Daniel. 1991. *Varieties of Social Explanation: An Introduction to the Philosophy of Social Science*. Boulder, CO: Westview.

Ljung, Lennart. 1987. *System Identification: Theory for the User*. Englewood Cliffs, NJ: Prentice Hall.

Mahoney, James, and Gary Goertz. 2006. "A Tale of Two Cultures: Contrasting Quantitative and Qualitative Research." *Political Analysis* 14 (3): 227–49.

Mäki, Uskali. 2009. "MISSing the World. Models as Isolations and Credible Surrogate Systems." *Erkenntnis* 70 (1): 29–43.

Maoz, Zeev, and Bruce Russett. 1993. "Normative and Structural Causes of Democratic Peace, 1946–1986." *American Political Science Review* 87 (3): 624–38.

Mari, Luca. 2007. "Measurability." In *Measurement in Economics: A Handbook*, ed. Marcel Boumans. London: Academic Press.

Martin, Andrew D., and Kevin M. Quinn. 2002. "Dynamic Ideal Point Estimation via Markov Chain Monte Carlo for the U.S. Supreme Court, 1953–1999." *Political Analysis* 10 (2): 134–53.

McCarty, Nolan M. 2000. "Presidential Pork: Executive Veto Power and Distributive Politics." 94 (1): 117–29.

McCullagh, Peter. 2002. "What Is a Statistical Model?" *Annals of Statistics* 30 (5): 1225–310.

McKeown, Timothy J. 2004. "Case Studies and the Limits of the Quantitative Worldview." In *Rethinking Social Inquiry*, ed. Henry E. Brady and David Collier. Lanham, MD: Rowman and Littlefield.

Mebane, Walter R. Jr., and Jasjeet S. Sekhon. 2002. "Coordination and Policy Moderation at Midterm." *American Political Science Review* 96 (1): 141–57.

Miller, John H., and Scott E. Page. 2007. *Complex Adaptive Systems: An Introduction to Computational Models of Social Life.* Princeton, NJ: Princeton University Press.

Milner, Helen V. 1997. *Interests, Institutions, and Information: Domestic Politics and International Relations.* Princeton, NJ: Princeton University Press.

Minogue, Brendan P. 1984. "Van Fraassen's Semanticism." *PSA: Proceedings of the Biennial Meeting of the Philosophy of Science Association* 1: 115–21.

Mittlehammer, Ron C., George G. Judge, and Douglas J. Miller. 2000. *Econometric Foundations.* New York: Cambridge University Press.

Mo, Jongryn. 1994. "The Logic of Two-Level Games with Endogenous Domestic Coalitions." *Journal of Conflict Resolution* 38 (3): 402–22.

Mo, Jongryn. 1995. "Domestic Institutions and International Bargaining: The Role of Agent Veto in Two-Level Games." *American Political Science Review* 89 (4): 914–24.

Moe, Terry M. 1989. "The Politics of Bureaucratic Structure." In *Can the Government Govern?*, ed. John E. Chubb and Paul E. Peterson. Washington, DC: Brookings Institution Press.

Monari, Paola. 1993. "Falsification or Choice among Alternatives: The Unsolved Dilemma of Hypothesis Testing." *Statistical Methods and Applications* 2 (3): 337–48.

Morrison, Margaret. 2005. "Approximating the Real: The Role of Idealizations in Physical Theory." In *Idealization XII: Correcting the Model–Idealization and Abstraction in the Sciences,* ed. Martin R. Jones and Nancy Cartwright. Amsterdam: Rodopi.

Morrison, Margaret, and Mary S. Morgan. 1999a. "Introduction." In *Models as Mediators: Perspectives on Natural and Social Science,* ed. Mary S. Morgan and Margaret Morrison. Cambridge: Cambridge University Press.

Morrison, Margaret, and Mary S. Morgan. 1999b. "Models as Mediating Instruments." In *Models as Mediators: Perspectives on Natural and Social Science,* ed. Mary S. Morgan and Margaret Morrison. Cambridge: Cambridge University Press.

Morton, Adam. 1993. "Mathematical Models: Questions of Trustworthiness." *British Journal for the Philosophy of Science* 44 (4): 659–74.

Morton, Rebecca B. 1999. *Methods and Models: A Guide to the Empirical Analysis of Formal Models in Political Science.* New York: Cambridge University Press.

National Science Foundation. 2002. "EITM: Empirical Implications of Theoretical Models Report." Publication of the Political Science Program.

Ordeshook, Peter C. 1986. *Game Theory and Political Theory: An Introduction.* Cambridge: Cambridge University Press.

Ostrom, Elinor. 1990. *Governing the Commons: The Evolution of Institutions for Collective Action.* New York: Cambridge University Press.

Overview. 2008. http://www.poli.duke.edu/eitm/overview.htm. Accessed August 22, 2008.

Pahre, Robert. 1997. "Endogenous Domestic Institutions in Two-Level Games and Parliamentary Oversight of the European Union." *Journal of Conflict Resolution* 41 (1): 147–74.

Pahre, Robert. 2005. "Formal Theory and Case-Study Methods in EU Studies." *European Union Politics* 6 (1): 113–45.

Perrow, Charles. 1999. *Normal Accidents: Living with High-Risk Technologies*. Princeton, NJ: Princeton University Press.

Pevehouse, Jon C. 2002. "Democracy from the Outside-In? International Organizations and Democratization." *International Organization* 56 (3): 515–49.

Pogrebin, Mark, ed. 2003. *Qualitative Approaches to Criminal Justice: Perspectives from the Field*. Thousand Oaks, CA: Sage.

Poole, Keith T., and Howard Rosenthal. 1985. "A Spatial Model for Legislative Roll Call Analysis." *American Journal of Political Science* 29 (2): 357–84.

Poole, Keith T., and Howard Rosenthal. 1991. "Patterns of Congressional Voting." *American Journal of Political Science* 35 (1): 228–78.

Popper, Karl R. 1968. *The Logic of Scientific Discovery*, 2nd ed. New York: Harper and Row.

Putnam, Hilary. 1991. "The 'Corroboration' of Theories." In *The Philosophy of Science*, ed. Richard Boyd, Philip Gasper, and J. D. Trout. Cambridge, MA: MIT Press.

Putnam, Robert D. 1988. "Diplomacy and Domestic Politics: The Logic of Two-Level Games." *International Organization* 42 (3): 427–60.

Quine, Willard Van Orman. 1951. "Two Dogmas of Empiricism." *Philosophical Review* 60 (1): 20–43.

Rappaport, Steven. 1998. *Models and Reality in Economics*. Cheltenham, UK: Edward Elgar.

Riker, William H. 1957. "Events and Situations." *Journal of Philosophy* 54 (3): 57–70.

Riker, William H. 1958. "Causes of Events." *Journal of Philosophy* 55 (7): 281–91.

Riker, William H. 1962. *The Theory of Political Coalitions*. New Haven, CT: Yale University Press.

Riker, William H. 1977. "The Future of a Science of Politics." *American Behavioral Scientist* 21 (1): 11–38.

Riker, William H. 1990. "Political Science and Rational Choice." In *Perspectives on Positive Political Economy*, ed. James E. Alt and Kenneth A. Shepsle. New York: Cambridge University Press.

Riker, William H., and Peter C. Ordeshook. 1968. "A Theory of the Calculus of Voting." *American Political Science Review* 62 (1): 25–42.

Romer, Thomas, and Howard Rosenthal. 1978. "Political Resource Allocation, Controlled Agendas, and the Status Quo." *Public Choice* 33 (4): 27–43.

Rosato, Sebastian. 2003. "The Flawed Logic of Democratic Peace Theory." *American Political Science Review* 97 (4): 585–602.

Rubinstein, Ariel. 2006. "Dilemmas of an Economic Theorist." *Econometrica* 74 (4): 865–83.

Sally, David. 1995. "Conversation and Cooperation in Social Dilemmas: A Meta-Analysis of Experiments from 1958–1992." *Rationality and Society* 7 (1): 58–92.

Salmon, Merrilee H., John Earman, Clark Glymour, James G. Lennox, Peter Machamer, J. E. McGuire, John D. Norton, Wesley C. Salmon, and Kenneth F. Schaffner. 1992. *Introduction to the Philosophy of Science.* Englewood Cliffs, NJ: Prentice Hall.

Salmon, Wesley C. 1971. *Statistical Explanation and Statistical Relevance.* Pittsburgh: University of Pittsburgh Press.

Salmon, Wesley C. 1984. *Scientific Explanation and the Causal Structure of the World.* Princeton, NJ: Princeton University Press.

Salmon, Wesley C. 1988. "Introduction." In *The Limitations of Deductivism*, ed. Adolf Grünbaum, and Wesley C. Salmon. Pittsburgh Series in Philosophy and History of Science. Berkeley: University of California Press.

Salmon, Wesley C. 1992. "Scientific Explanation." In *Introduction to the Philosophy of Science.* Englewood Cliffs, NJ: Prentice Hall.

Salmon, Wesley C. 1998. *Causality and Explanation.* New York: Oxford University Press.

Satterthwaite, Mark A. 1975. "Strategy-Proofness and Arrow's Conditions: Existence and Correspondence Theorems for Voting Procedures and Social Welfare Functions." *Journal of Economic Theory* 10 (2): 187–217.

Schaffner, Kenneth F. 1969. "Correspondence Rules." *Philosophy of Science* 36 (3): 280–90.

Schelling, Thomas C. 1978. *Micromotives and Macrobehavior.* New York: Norton.

Scriven, Michael. 1959. "Explanation and Prediction in Evolutionary Theory." *Science* 130 (3374): 477–82.

Seawright, Jason. 2002. "Testing for Necessary and/or Sufficient Causation: Which Cases Are Relevant?" *Political Analysis* 10 (2): 178–93.

Sellars, Wilfrid. 1956. "Is There a Synthetic A Priori?" In *American Philosophers at Work: The Philosophical Scene in the United States*, ed. Sidney Hook. New York: Criterion Books.

Selten, Reinhard, and Rolf Stoecker. 1986. "End Behavior in Sequences of Finite Prisoner's Dilemma Supergames: A Learning Theory Approach." *Journal of Economic Behavior and Organization* 7 (1): 47–70.

Shepsle, Kenneth A. 1995. "Statistical Political Philosophy and Positive Political Theory." *Critical Review* 9 (1 and 2): 213–22.

Shepsle, Kenneth A., and Barry R. Weingast. 1987. "The Institutional Foundations of Committee Power." *American Political Science Review* 81 (1): 85–104.

Shipan, Charles R. 1996. "Senate Committees and Turf: Do Jurisdictions Matter?" *Political Research Quarterly* 49 (1): 177–89.

Shipan, Charles R. 2004. "Regulatory Regimes, Agency Actions, and the Conditional Nature of Congressional Influence." *American Political Science Review* 98 (3): 467–80.

Shleifer, Andrei, and Robert W. Vishny. 1993. "Corruption." *Quarterly Journal of Economics* 108 (3): 599–617.

Signorino, Curtis S. 1999. "Strategic Interaction and the Statistical Analysis of International Conflict." *American Political Science Review* 93 (2): 279–97.

Singer, J. David, and Melvin Small. 1972. *The Wages of War, 1816–1965.* New York: Wiley.

Sloep, Peter B., and Wim J. van der Steen. 1987. "The Nature of Evolutionary Theory: The Semantic Challenge." *Biology and Philosophy* 2 (1): 1–15.

Snyder, James M. Jr., Michael M. Ting, and Stephen Ansolabehere. 2005. "Legislative Bargaining under Weighted Voting." *American Economic Review* 95 (4): 981–1004.

Spanos, Aris. 1999. *Probability Theory and Statistical Inference: Econometric Modeling with Observational Data.* New York: Cambridge University Press.

Stibitz, George R. 1966. *Mathematics in Medicine and the Sciences.* Chicago: Year Book Medical.

Stigum, Bernt P. 2003. *Econometrics and the Philosophy of Economics: Theory-Data Confrontations in Economics.* Princeton, NJ: Princeton University Press.

Sugden, Robert. 2001. "Credible Worlds: The Status of Theoretical Models in Economics." *Journal of Economic Methodology* 7 (1): 1–31.

Suppe, Frederick. 1977. *The Structure of Scientific Theories,* 2nd ed. Chicago: University of Illinois Press.

Suppe, Frederick. 1989. *The Semantic Conception of Theories and Scientific Realism.* Chicago: University of Illinois Press.

Suppe, Frederick. 2000. "Understanding Scientific Theories: An Assessment of Developments, 1969–1998." *Philosophy of Science* 67 (Supplement): S102–S115.

Suppes, Patrick. 1961. "A Comparison of the Meaning and Uses of Models in Mathematics and the Empirical Science." In *The Concept and Role of the Model in Mathematics and Natural and Social Sciences,* ed. H. Freudenthal. Dordrecht, Holland: Reidel.

Suppes, Patrick. 1967. "What Is a Scientific Theory?" In *Philosophy of Science Today,* ed. Sidney Morgenbesser. New York: Basic Books.

Tarski, Alfred. 1953. "A General Method in Proofs of Undecidability." *Studies in Logic and the Foundations of Mathematics* 13: 1–34.

Tetlock, Philip E., and Aaron Belkin, eds. 1996a. *Counterfactual Thought Experiments in World Politics: Logical, Methodological, and Psychological Perspectives.* Princeton, NJ: Princeton University Press.

Tetlock, Philip E., and Aaron Belkin, eds. 1996b. "Counterfactual Thought Experiments in World Politics." In *Counterfactual Thought Experiments in World Politics: Logical, Methodological, and Psychological Perspectives*, ed. Philip E. Tetlock and Aaron Belkin. Princeton, NJ: Princeton University Press.

Theil, Henri. 1971. *Principles of Econometrics*. New York: Wiley.

Thompson, Paul. 1989. *The Structure of Biological Theories*. Albany: State University of New York Press.

Treier, Shawn, and Simon Jackman. 2008. "Democracy as a Latent Variable." *American Journal of Political Science* 52 (1): 201–17.

Van Evera, Stephen. 1997. *Guide to Methods for Students of Political Science*. Ithaca, NY: Cornell University Press.

van Fraassen, Bas C. 1972. "A Formal Approach to the Philosophy of Science." In *Paradigms and Paradoxes: The Philosophical Challenge of the Quantum Domain*, ed. Robert G. Colodny. Pittsburgh: University of Pittsburgh Press.

van Fraassen, Bas C. 1980. *The Scientific Image*. New York: Oxford University Press.

van Fraassen, Bas C. 1989. *Laws and Symmetry*. New York: Oxford University Press.

van Fraassen, Bas C. 2008. *Scientific Representation: Paradoxes of Perspective*. New York: Oxford University Press.

Vuong, Quang. 1989. "Likelihood Ratio Tests for Model Selection and Non-Nested Hypotheses." *Econometrica* 57 (2): 307–33.

Weingast, Barry R. 1979. "A Rational Choice Perspective on Congressional Norms." *American Journal of Political Science* 23 (2): 245–62.

Weingast, Barry R., Kenneth A. Shepsle, and Christopher Johnsen. 1981. "The Political Economy of Benefits and Costs: A Neoclassical Approach to Distributive Politics." *Journal of Political Economy* 89 (4): 642–64.

Wendt, Alexander. 1992. "Anarchy Is What States Make of It: The Social Construction of Power Politics." *International Organization* 46 (2): 391–425.

Wooldridge, Jeffrey M. 2002. *Econometric Analysis of Cross Section and Panel Data*. Cambridge, MA: MIT Press.

Wright, Quincy. 1942. *A Study of War*, vol. 1. Chicago: University of Chicago Press.

Zaller, John R. 1992. *The Nature and Origins of Mass Opinion*. New York: Cambridge University Press.

Zupan, Mark A. 1991. "An Economic Explanation for the Existence and Nature of Political Ticket Splitting." *Journal of Law and Economics* 34 (2): 343–69.

SUBJECT INDEX